SALMON TAKING TIMES

SALMON TAKING TIMES

R.V. RIGHYNI

SWAN·HILL
PRESS

Copyright © 1965 R. V. Righyni

First published in the UK in 1965
by Macdonald and Company (Publishers) Ltd

This edition published 1996
by Swan Hill Press, an imprint of Airlife Publishing Ltd

British Library Cataloguing in Publication Data
  A catalogue record for this book
  is available from the British Library

ISBN 1 85310 760 3

Typeset by Hewer Text Composition Services Ltd
Printed in England by Livesey Ltd, Shrewsbury

Swan Hill Press
an imprint of Airlife Publishing Ltd
101 Longden Road, Shrewsbury SY3 9EB, England

Introduction

By Bernard Venables

I recall that first meeting well; I remember still the sense of impact. I had gone to Yorkshire to attend the Annual Dinner of the Bradford Waltonians, and there, Terry Thomas told me, I would meet R. V. Righyni. He had told me of him before, roused expectation in me, and then, on this night, I met him; the next day we, Righyni, Terry Thomas and I, went to the Lune to fish. It was the first time I had fished the Lune and the first time I had fished with Reg Righyni; this was a memorable coincidence of events.

He talked as he drove, following the tortuous road from Ilkley over the Pennines to Kirkby Lonsdale, talked and drove the Bristol with a masterful skill that, I was to learn, was essential to him. He talked a little of cars and driving, but mostly he talked of fishing, and particularly of salmon fishing. I have never seen salmon fishing in the same way since. There was a sense of revelation – not of one new idea, one new aspect, but of a tumbling torrent of fresh conceptions. It was my first experience of the fact that Reg Righyni is a man who cannot accept anything just as he finds it, with mute unquestioning; he must probe restlessly, enquire, examine, quest with a lancet of logic. It was, at this first impact, an unsettling experience; I fished that day as if it was the first on which I had touched a rod. Others, I understand, have been similarly affected.

When first the wave of his thought broke over me, it was

5

formless, and I floundered in the surge of it; but then, and
subsequently, I gained a purchase on it. A pattern came, and
then I learned of the Theory. It has been difficult since then to
remember how I had seen salmon fishing before – or, indeed,
fishing as a whole. It is so it works; so it worked on me, so,
Terry Thomas told me, it had worked on him. Righyni told
me the theory, explained it, and I listened – almost silently,
I think it must have been – and I suppose I was startled.
But then the idea of it settled, coalesced, became, as it
were, almost obsessionally convincing. It made everything
in past fishing experience suddenly all of one pattern; it gave
relationship to all. It was the lucidity, the reasonableness
it gave remembered experience, and indeed all current
experience, that was so sweepingly convincing. Though
we continued to talk of The Theory, I suppose that from
that first time of acceptance of it I have never again thought
of it as a theory. I think that every time I have been fishing
since there has been further confirmation – this is a theory to
explain the behaviour of salmon because it was the problems
of salmon fishing with which Righyni was preoccupied, but
it throws no less clear a light on the behaviour of other
fish. It goes indeed beyond that, gives explanation for all
the animal behaviour that is related to our fishing, makes
rational and demonstrable all the lore that we, and all the
fishermen before us, have been guided by. We have liked
the 'soft day'; we have disliked the dry lacking-in-humidity
easterly blowing day. We have responded, we have seen
all river valley life respond, to just those conditions that, R.
V. Righyni now demonstrates, are those of optimum oxygen
availability. We have seen the sudden hatches of fly on April
trouting days, suddenly starting, suddenly ending; we have
seen the different pattern of fly hatches on days of late
spring. We have, all of us sometimes, cogitated on this. Now
read this book, and read it again because it may hardly be
entirely assimilated in one reading, and then consider again
the hatching behaviour of flies.

The book must be classically memorable for the oxygen theory alone, but its revelation is no less startling otherwise. We have all, when we have fished long enough, watched water long enough, formed a generalised idea of its behaviour; but that idea has usually been rather superficial, partly empirical. It has not given us so universal, so theoretical an understanding of the mechanics of running water and of salmon that we could go with certainty to a strange water and pick out the lies that will hold fish. Has it not indeed been said, many times, that salmon fishing differed in this respect from trout fishing, that in salmon fishing, unlike trout fishing, there is no substitute for local knowledge of where fish lie? So it has been, and now, so suddenly, in this book there is given us so rational, so lucid an analysis of the mechanical behaviour of rivers and of the salmon's responses to that behaviour that there is no theoretical reason why we should not go to any strange river and make a sufficiently successful reading of it to know with certainty where fish will be lying in whatever conditions are current. 'Yes,' you may say, 'no *theoretical* reason; but, how often is theory really going to become fact?' To answer that doubt let an illustration be given. Righyni was coming south to fish as my guest on the Hampshire Avon. Till then all his very wide experience of salmon fishing had been on what we normally regard as typical salmon rivers, such rivers as his own Lune, the rivers of Scotland. The Avon is like none of these; it is a chalk stream, heavily weeded, with a fast heavy flow that is, by contrast with those other rivers, even. It lacks the pattern of rumpled rapid, stream, run, deep steady dub, and then a glide before the next pool below. It is, as Righyni said on seeing it, nearly all glide. It is, apparently, and has always been said to be, a more or less irreconcilably different problem from typical salmon rivers. It has also been declared persistently that it is no river for the fly fisher; spinning has been the nearly universal method. We fished on a rather hot June day with a rather low river; there was no more cloud than a sparse and lazy drift of fluffy white. Righyni fished only fly. 'I don't think,' he said, 'that we shall have a fish until about 5 o'clock.'

But we fished through the day, conscientiously, not trying the less for that prophecy; and Reg Righyni made his own analysis of the water as we moved down. On one pool, a particularly enchanting one, he said that he thought the best lie in the whole pool was one quite small area of a glide towards the tail, just where the bough of an overhanging tree was low over the water. In the three seasons I had fished the water it had been at that place, in this very prolific pool, that I had seen most fish move. But now it was still hot mid-afternoon, and we moved down.

Approaching 5 o'clock we were fishing down a long pool that ended with a glide that swung diagonally across the river. Reg Righyni drew my attention to a particular place in the glide, giving me bearings from either side, pinpointing the place. 'There will be a fish there' he said, and then, a little later, just about 5 o'clock, at that place he was taken with a beautiful head-and-tail rise. 15 lb. the fish went.

Theory then, can be practice; but this is not to suggest that you will read this book and, at once, so effectively translate its teaching into success as certain as that. You will, I foresee, need re-readings of the book, coming back to it to refer to it actual problems of water as they are met. It will be by such degrees of practical application that full grasp of its theories will grow. And, indeed, and fortunately for the continuance of the delight of fishing, you will never cease to find new variants of what it postulates. You will, incidentally, have made a good start when you apply Righyni's dictum, so obvious once he has pointed it out, that a river should be looked at from downstream. It is only thus that its anatomy can be clearly seen – how clearly may be a revelation when it is first tried.

That part of the book which deals with flies is in logical and proper sequence to the rest. It shows the same entire freedom from shiboleth, the same, so to speak, unfettered capacity to take from the past what illuminates his new thinking of the present. How lambently past experience is translated into reasoned principle as we read, and by degrees fully absorb, Righyni's analysis of the way a salmon sees a fly – sees it in all the variants of water, weather, and light. 'Ah yes, of course' we say as he translates that into patterns of artificial flies.

I will say quite boldly that I think that this book will be called a classic; I am sure that, seen in retrospect, it will be in that line which includes Stewart's *The Practical Angler*, Dunn's *Sunshine and The Dry Fly*, Skues' *Minor Tactics of The Chalkstream*. It is a book, like those, that once having been read, permanently changes the reader's way of seeing the kind of fishing that it deals with. Salmon fishing, it has so often been declared, is something that any fool can do; when the fish really are on, so the saying is, catching them demands no skill. In that very minor part of the salmon's period in freshwater after return from the sea when it *is* so recklessly 'on', then it is true that any fool can catch it; this book is for the benefit of those who fish for salmon during the other and vastly greater part of the time when the consistent catching of them demands great skill and experience. It is for the benefit of those (the majority of us) who have to take the river as they find it when they have the chance to fish for salmon, and do so feeling that they have reasonable hope of catching salmon. It is also for the benefit of those of whom it might be said that they are convinced salmon fishermen; by that I mean that they do not take a highly priced beat on the best parts of such rivers as Dee and Spey and Tay and Tweed at the best time of the season, but instead fish out the whole season for salmon, as a trout fisher does for trout. They follow through the whole season's sequence in big cold waters and shrunken summer ones. They accept the fascination of the challenge that every modulation of water and weather brings throughout the salmon season.

The close reasoning, the cool logic, that this book has – and as other books of its rare kind have had – may suggest that its author brings to fishing a laboratory detachment, that he does not feel the emotional responses that the rest of us do, does not have all those moments of delighted awareness that make up the passage of a fishing day. Nothing could be less true; Reg Righyni is as emotionally involved as the rest of us. He is indeed as wholly good a fishing companion as I have ever known.

Preface

In the days before the allure of the salmon became too compelling for me to afford time for other pursuits, I used to like to arrive at a trout-stream comfortably in advance of the hatches of fly. I was very content waiting for the first duns to appear, and to see the beginning of the rise was a great satisfaction.

Everything was too wonderful to miss any part of it. I felt sorry for late-comers who tried hurriedly to make the most of what remained of the opportunity for sport; sometimes they spoilt their fishing by their haste.

But this feeling of having the situation well in hand was quite absent at the beginning of a day's salmon fishing. If conditions appeared to be favourable, and I fished for a spell without getting any response, I began to suspect that the fish were in one of their disinterested moods; how long, I wondered, should I have to keep at it for the chance of something happening. On the other hand, if there was a rise to my fly at an early stage, I became apprehensive that this, perhaps, was the closing phase of a good taking period. Having missed most of it, should I have to spend the rest of the day casting to uncatchable fish?

This perplexity was nearly always present to some degree, and conversation with other anglers revealed that I did not suffer such thoughts alone.

To make a fairly reliable assessment of prospects in spring, when conditions are seasonable, and the pools well stocked with fresh-run fish, does not need much experience. Such occasions are not nearly as common as we would hope though, and when – much more frequently – there were peculiar combinations of weather and water, I found that I simply could not judge reliably.

I became very intrigued by reports of anglers reputed to have a sixth sense about the moods of the salmon. But, eventually, I was able to satisfy myself that many thus thought to have this deeper understanding were, indeed, not more than extremely good anglers with vast experience. Their method remained, however, one of rule-of-thumb, despite its usefulness. They could be very helpful, very instructive, but they neither claimed secret knowledge nor freedom from the fear that the fish might not behave as they expected. They made no apology for their reserve; just make one confident prediction, they said, and at once a situation might arise to show how little one really knows.

Nevertheless, I do not deny that people do exist who can recognise instinctively and accurately the circumstances of weather and water in which fish will take, and, probably, anticipate such occasions in the short term. It seems to me, though, that they must have quite extraordinary physical sensitiveness, and must rely upon it almost entirely. Surely if those people who can "smell" when it is the right time to fish, rare though they are, were capable of revealing their means on an elementary, abstract basis, for the benefit of the less gifted, they would have done so.

This realisation made me feel terribly frustrated for some time; but I remained convinced that salmon taking times were not purely haphazard as so many people assert. They *must* occur as a result of positive material and physical factors.

Disregarding the risk that I should achieve nothing more than to irritate myself still further, I decided to attempt a study of all the possibly relevant factors I could discover. High precedence, naturally, was given to such things as I had learned about the general conditions common to those times when sport is good, and, particularly, any features which appeared common to the different classes of taking times.

For a long time I was lost in instrument readings, and, having had no training for it, I was very slow to see any interrelation of the principal factors. I had no sudden inspirations; but, gradually, a pattern seemed to be evolving, and eventually I became conscious of a feeling that the probable solution was only eluding me because of my lack of wit to see the obvious.

For a few more seasons this went on, and I was encouraged by an increasing success in anticipating the taking times – despite the annoying gaps in the formula I was using. Then, one lucky day, I observed a sequence of activities by some salmon which gave me the clue that had been missing.

Several months of fascinating trial followed. I became bold enough to start predicting to friends the approximate time of day when they would catch a salmon, if at all. I had ample grounds for satisfaction with the results.

This then, several years ago, gave me the confidence to explain the theory to an internationally famous angler and author. He was interested immediately and, quite quickly, became enthusiastic. The number of supporters is now considerable, and, so far, nobody has come out into open opposition.

A good friend of mine, very well known for his writing on angling and exceptional fly-fishing skill, invited me to collaborate with him in the writing of a comprehensive work on salmon fishing. I should have been proud to be associated with him, but I felt that practical fishing for salmon is already well covered in many books. It would be better, I thought, if I were to restrict myself to a few of the problems which I have found particularly interesting and which do not appear to have been dealt with as fully as many of my angling acquaintances tell me they would wish.

I should like to say that I am very much aware that my

layman's view of points which are in the province of the scientist might well be inaccurate: nobody will be more happy than I to have the criticism and correction of the specialist. Then results of my observations might be a more reliable help towards increasing the satisfaction that is to be had from fishing for salmon.

Captain T. B. Thomas (Terry Thomas to his countless friends) is widely acknowledged to have a genius for putting his finger – as delicately or otherwise as the situation demands – on any flaw or inconsistency in any idea about fishing. His general support for my views – after a great deal of critical thought – has therefore been invaluable encouragement to me throughout the preparation of this work. And his enthusiasm for the book has given me the necessary confidence that his interest will be shared by other salmon fishers. For this and his unfailing help and friendship, I wish to express my deep gratitude to Terry Thomas.

I wish to thank Michael Prichard for all the photographs except the last one, for which I am indebted to Arthur Oglesby. On the colour plates of the flies, the feather-wing patterns were dressed by 'Farlows'. (The hair-wing flies are my own tying.)

Finally I wish to thank Bernard Venables most sincerely for his invaluable help with the MS., for the line drawings which illustrate this book, and for his innumerable other acts of great generosity.

Contents

SALMON TAKING TIMES

Salmon Taking Times

When and why salmon take

Let us start by reviewing what is generally, ordinarily, known of the specific periods when ready response can be expected from the salmon.

When a fish has been running and eventually reaches a pool in which he is going to be a resident for anything from one or two days up to a few weeks, he will often announce his arrival by showing on the surface, and take a brief look around before settling down. When he has selected his lie, if he is shown a reasonably suitable lure, he will seldom refuse it.

But, were that same salmon left undisturbed that day, and then during the course of the following day he were offered a fly or bait at intervals of, say, half an hour, the chances are that he would ignore everything he saw on several of those occasions. Eventually he would take, probably so boldly that one would think that the successful lure were just what he had been waiting for all his life. This period during which it would not be difficult to interest him would be limited, however; afterwards he would again become unresponsive.

Next, we know that if we cover a fish around the time when a run is about to start, he is nearly certain to be a taker. Once it has started and he resumes his journey up the river, there is not much hope of getting him to look at anything. So it is until he feels the need for a little breather, and settles for a while in a resting place – as he would do, for instance, after negotiating a long stretch of very tough going. If he sees a fly or bait during that short halt, he is much more likely than not to have a go at it.

Eventually, having got as far upstream as his involuntary desire dictates for the time being, he surveys his new temporary home as before, and the same sequence starts again.

From this we establish that just before and just after a move, and during the rest taken when travelling, the salmon is in a responsive mood. And it will be agreed that on each of these occasions the fish is in much the same state of physical and mental alertness.

As yet, though, there is no apparent basic similarity between those three situations and the taking times which occur when a fish is resident in a pool. But we shall see the existence of some such relationship if we consider what causes a fish to run and determines the distances which he can travel during a particular journey.

For this purpose we must first turn to the situation when the salmon re-enters the river from the sea. The stomach is atrophied, and the body is a wonderful reservoir of concentrated energy-providing substances derived from lush saltwater feeding. With nothing more than the oxygen absorbed through its respiratory organs, this reserve is sufficient to give the salmon the strength to survive during its stay in fresh water – and that may be for as long as upwards of a year. During that time it will cover distances upstream of up to one hundred miles or more, and its store of energy must also provide for the development of a relatively huge amount of milt or ova.

The only apparent external factor in the salmons' needs, then, is their requirement of oxygen.

Both the demand for oxygen, and the supply of it, vary considerably. The rate of metabolism of the salmon requires a variably but progressively increasing intake up to spawning time; the availability of oxygen at any one point in the river is ceaselessly changing because of the many influences which affect it.

The scientists tell us that the water of a salmon river, with good aeration and no pollution, is capable of containing more dissolved oxygen when its temperature is low than when it is higher, but that in cold water the respiratory organs of the fish have more difficulty in extracting the oxygen than is the case in less cold water. Therefore, up to a point, rising temperature of the water means to the fish an increasing supply of oxygen because they are able to get at it. Throughout the fishing season that is a most important matter for consideration. But the full statement of the position would be that the *availability* of oxygen to the fish is dependent upon the varying degree of *accessibility* of a varying *actual amount* dissolved in the water. Consequently it could be that the poor accessibility of a large amount, as in the early part of the season when the water is cold, may produce a greater availability than would be the case when, in the warm water of hot weather, there is great accessibility to the low-oxygen content.

In addition to this factor of the temperature of the water, aquatic vegetation gives off oxygen in sunlight. During the hours of darkness, carbon-dioxide is produced. So, as the day advances to its warmest point, the tendency is for there to be a continuous improvement in the ease with which the fish can satisfy their need of oxygen.

Without there being any possibility of assessing it (or need to, for that matter), on either side of the exact amount of oxygen which would suit a fish best there is obviously a margin of tolerance which will satisfy it reasonably well. The fish, of course, is master itself of quite a lot of variation. All it has to do is to move a yard or two into faster or slower water, and thereby make many of the adjustments which it needs.

There comes a time, however, when the fish senses that soon no position in its temporary home will be

21

capable of matching its oxygen requirements throughout the twenty-four hours, and soon it must move higher up the river. Usually the need is sufficiently flexible for the fish to be able to await the help of a spate; but, if that does not occur in time, it will struggle up the river as best it can – but that should be regarded as abnormal. In times of drought it may have to remain in a pool and endure real suffering and, sadly, sometimes the ordeal is fatal.

The salmon chooses the spate for its running, as it usually does when it re-enters fresh water from the sea, for the obvious reason, among others, that the river is then more easily negotiable. It can find just that speed of current which is most helpful to good progress with the minimum of effort on its part.

A much more vital inducement, though, is the fact that when in spate the water is in its most stable state in respect of the availability of oxygen, with less tendency to variation. Neither sun nor wind can have much effect on the temperature of that big volume of rapidly flowing water. Stretches that produce maximum aeration at normal level are covered by heavy swirls; the greatest variation in the production of oxygen or carbon-dioxide by aquatic plants is, in those circumstances, of no importance.

When the spate comes then, if the availability of oxygen matches the salmon's requirements for running, and it feels the urge to do so, it senses that it can rely on this availability lasting long enough for it to travel a long distance. The risk of finding itself compelled to stop semi-permanently in an undesirable place is at a minimum.

From this we can see that the taking times of the fish just before starting to run, during the halts when travelling, and after the completion of the journey, all occur with the oxygen supply at substantially the same level.

Now we will consider how those three situations compare with, and can be equivalent to, the times when the salmon is settled in a pool and becomes, for a period, responsive to the angler.

We will take a normal spring or early summer day with conditions in all respects quite reasonable for fishing. We can assume that the oxygen supply within the chosen lie of the fish is acceptable throughout the twenty-four hours. But we also know that there is considerable difference in the accessibility of oxygen during the hours of darkness and during the warmest part of the day.

It is, I believe, when the increasing availability of oxygen reaches a critical point as the day progresses that the salmon's mood becomes responsive. It is at that same critical point that the fish would start to run if it needed to do so, and other water conditions were suitable.

As the increase in oxygen availability continues, it becomes excessive for the comfortable requirements of the fish, and it goes off the take. Sometimes then it is only necessary for it to lie quietly to avoid too great an intake; but there are occasions when it has to seek deep, slow water to escape a dangerous over-supply. Later, as the temperature of the water declines, the gradual reduction of accessibility commences, and, once more, when it reaches a certain level, the fish will take again. (No doubt the resultant pattern of taking times is what inspired the famous eleven o'clock and four o'clock theory, which I support fully – provided that it is used with suitable flexibility.)

The salmon being cold-blooded, we accept that it has no appreciation of temperature changes in terms of warmth or coldness; but it seems safe to assume that the influence of temperature changes on oxygen availability do give it physical sensations.

When a taking time arrives, I think it is because the salmon feels a surge of energy which brings him to his peak of physical and mental alertness. While he is in that state and sees from his lie something reminiscent of the prey of his feeding days, either in the sea or perhaps as a parr, reflex action makes him move to take it. At all other times, it seems that the angler's lure simply does not engender in him the hunting instinct, and the fly, spinner, or bait looks uninteresting and as useless to him as it actually is. (On occasions, of course, it will appear to him to be dangerous.)

That, I submit, establishes the cause which is common to all occasions ,when the salmon involuntarily comes on the take – a specific level of availability of oxygen for the salmon on an individual basis – remembering, of course, that there can be many individuals which are alike.

Few days are free from weather peculiarities which cause variations in the times when the fish will come on to the take, in the duration of the activity, and in the number of occasions when such an event will occur. But I consider that the days when the fish, even potted ones, do not come on to the take at all are relatively few – certainly not nearly so numerous as the majority of anglers seem to think.

Sometimes a very skilled angler can catch a salmon in a way that some readers will probably think is a definite contradiction of the foregoing. I refer to the occasion when conditions are extremely unfavourable, and a fish which is known to be in a certain lie is pestered until it takes a spinner. I think that that fish acts voluntarily, out of a sense of fear – the need to protect itself against the menacing creature which persistently threatens it: and this should not be confused with the take of a fish during a period of good sport, when, as I have said, I believe that the response is largely involuntary. I also think that in preference to defending itself by taking the bait to destroy it, such a fish would always move away to another lie if it were possible to do so: and that salmon can only be taken in that manner when the circumstances are such that the danger that a departure from the lie would involve is greater than that of remaining where it is and coping with the challenge of the bait.

Perhaps it will also be thought that when a salmon behaves in a manner which suggests that hunger is inducing the voluntary taking of a bait, such as a worm, it is inconsistent with the oxygen theory. I think there is convincing proof that it is not so. If the salmon actually had an appetite for food in fresh water (which would be a most unkind and useless thing for nature to permit), it would seem that it would necessarily be constant, because, the stomach being atrophied, the normal function which creates the desire to feed is absent. But the salmon certainly has not got a constant appetite, a fact demonstrated by its frequent complete lack of interest in worms and so on. The suggestion is often heard that it takes a worm in order to extract the juices before discarding the chewed-up pieces; I dispute this. It does not need the juices, and that seems to me to be a totally insufficient inducement. It does seem that it takes the worm voluntarily, but if indeed that is so, it is, surely, simply to destroy it out of aggressive resentment of the intrusion into the vicinity of its lie. But, when the availability of oxygen is on the low side for its requirements, it lies quietly to conserve its energy. Whether or not the resentment of the intrusion is still present, it cannot afford the exercise of aggressive behaviour. When the oxygen level is above its requirements, again it avoids unnecessary activity which would be harmful. I think that there is no doubt that the response of salmon to worms and other natural baits is restricted to periods when the availability of oxygen is suitable for general sport.

Why then, it may be asked, is it sometimes possible to take salmon on natural baits when artificial lures seem to be useless? The obvious answer is that the latter have to create the illusion of some natural prey of the fish, and to achieve this requires either the assistance of water current and perhaps surface disturbance, or extremely skilful manipulation on the part of the angler. The natural bait requires no assistance of that sort, and particularly if it is alive, as the worm is. It does not lose its essential identity from the salmon's point of view, even if it is anchored to the bottom of the river.

Another point is that anglers using natural bait usually confine themselves to lies which are definitely known to be occupied by salmon, and, consequently, are much more likely than the fly fisher or spinner to have the advantage of a taking time of very short duration. The fly fisher and the spinner may well not be actually covering fish during that little critical spell.

I hope that those words will not give the novice encouragement to less desirable activities. To fly fish, and sometimes spin, is, by general agreement, better sport. Most salmon rivers, fortunately, when in reasonably good order, give better, more regular, easier success to those who use those methods than to those who ignore them.

No doubt other arguments which I cannot anticipate will arise against full acceptance of my assessment of taking times; but I am sure that the reader, when fully familiar with the theory, will find that it fits all kinds of salmon fishing experiences of his own. I admit that sometimes the real obstacle to sport is only recognised in retrospect; natural optimism tends to make one play down sinister features and expect too much from the favourable ones. But this has its compensation in that one becomes very quick to appreciate the position when everything is favourable, and then one fishes with zest and enjoys everything to the full.

Those fortunate people who, living close to their salmon fishing and having a good information service, can pop down to the river at very short notice are probably chiefly interested in sport which is closely allied to the running of fish, and thus take such a big toll that they do not worry much about the established residents in the pools. Such anglers, on the lower reaches, are usually so familiar with the scheme of events that they find no difficulty in so timing their fishing that they are on the spot to greet the fresh-run fish as they arrive. Their success is such that they have little or no interest in new ideas and recourse to books; they are content to fish much as their grandfathers did.*

On the higher reaches the local rods have little to learn about the prospects of new fish reaching their beats and additionally they exploit to the fullest extent the taking times just before the fish begin to run again. Having immediate information on the state of the water and weather, they rarely fail to be in the right place when the river is affected by rain and the right time comes to catch the fish just before they would otherwise depart. They also have their favourite, well-tried places, where, with the river in spate and most of the salmon on the move, they can find a resting fish.

It often arouses curious comment from visitors when, on a nice suitable-looking day, with the river at a normal but still interesting level, the local rodsmen are otherwise engaged. But perhaps it is not surprising that such circumstances have little charm for those who know so well more hectic sport.

The city-dweller and holiday fisherman must be very lucky ever to participate in those exciting events. Their trips are fixed in advance, and when they do come to the water their fishing must usually be directed at resident salmon – what the locals would call potted fish. These visiting anglers are very greatly in the majority; and it is to this majority can come the greatest benefit from being able to make a good assessment of the position when they reach the river. To be able to anticipate such taking times as may occur is a very great help indeed. Without such help they may squander their energy when there is little chance of a fish, and then, when they should be starting to fish, they, dispirited, will be packing up. And, without this help, they

* See Commentary A.

may spend too much time admiring the fish they have just caught, or even stopping for lunch when they should be fishing on. Perhaps most important of all, it will save them from loss of faith in their flies, their tackle and their skill on days the hopelessness of which would not otherwise have been apparent.

Anticipating taking times

The problem, it will be appreciated, is to assess if and when the availability of oxygen will pass, upward or downward, through the phase in which the salmon will become responsive.

This is really very much more simple than a survey of the influences and factors which may be involved would suggest. Anglers are naturally interested in the elements and the features of the state of the river, and it only requires a little practice to become familiar with what has to be done.

It should be an encouragement too to realise that, excepting in the extremes of weather and water conditions, the level of oxygen availability is never far from that which is suitable for good sport. The change which will tip the scale, and which has to be foreseen, is, therefore, not very great.

Nor should the reader be put off by the number of items which have to be considered, and the apparently complicated way in which some of them are inter-related. In the end there are really only two decisions to be made. Firstly, will the temperature of the water rise or fall? Secondly, will other circumstances help or hinder the oxygen accessibility?

It is very seldom that, as the day progresses, the temperature of the air will not be sufficiently higher than that of the water to bring about a suitable increase if other factors will permit it. What we have to watch for more than anything else, perhaps, is evaporation and the consequent loss of heat at the surface of the water. Too much evaporation

28

prevents or nullifies the beneficial influence of warm air and hot sunshine, and it is, of course, the dryness of the air which causes evaporation. Therefore, the chief assessment we have to make is whether or not the degree of humidity of the atmosphere is such as to prevent the too great evaporation which would not allow the external warmth to influence the water.

The only other factor which we have to consider, which influences the degree of *accessibility* of any given amount of dissolved oxygen in the water at any given temperature, is the atmospheric pressure. Low pressure, it seems, facilitates the accessibility, high pressure hinders it.

It is quite unnecessary to become involved with instrument readings; very soon it will be found that one's own judgment can be adequate. An idea of the *trend* shown by the hygrometer, barometer, and thermometer is a useful guide; but specific measurements are of no value. We cannot hope to discover any constant for the amount of dissolved oxygen in the water, nor the required degree of its accessibility to the salmon to bring them on to the take. No actual figures, therefore, can reveal any indication of the proximity of a taking period.

To reiterate, all we want to know is whether the trend is such that the unknown availability will probably pass through the equally unknown bracket which produces sport. So long as we can judge that successfully, our ignorance of the specific equation will cost us nothing materially, and will ensure that the charm of salmon fishing remains unimpaired.

There are many peculiar manifestations of weather conditions and their trends that interest us, and these can be very helpful. We are familiar with most of them because they are the basis of so many of the old and well-tried sayings about natural phenomena and their probable influence on sport, and these will be considered shortly.

Simply by observations of the main pointers, then, we

form our opinion on the probable developments of the temperature of the water and the influence of the atmospheric pressure. This gives us our view of the trend of the accessibility of oxygen to the salmon. From that we decide whether any chances of sport which we foresee will be earlier or later than what we regard as normal for the state of the river at the particular time of the year.

The novice should be acquainted with the general outline of the changing times of the day, throughout the season, when salmon can reasonably be expected to be caught in favourable circumstances. In January we cannot expect good sport before about eleven o'clock in the morning, or much after half-past two in the afternoon. The valuable part of the day widens as the daylight lengthens and it becomes warmer. Eventually, in the latter part of spring, the early afternoon tends to get too hot, and a gap appears in the period of probable sport. This gap then grows until, in high summer, it can occupy the whole of the middle of the day; then only the very early morning and the evening are really promising times for fishing. As the autumn comes along, the unproductive gap narrows again, and, ultimately, closes, leaving us looking for sport with the autumn-run fish in late October and November at much the same time as we started off with the springers.

Of course, the variations in the weather at all seasons, which we experience in these islands, result in many disappointments and surprises if we fish to the seasonal time programme without modification. It is to make these needful adjustments that is our objective, so that we can take advantage of what would otherwise be unexpected and probably missed periods of sport.

The principal weather and water factors

A helpful perspective of the weather is given by remembering that, had this planet insufficient atmosphere, there would be a great intensification of the heat by day and the cold by night. The air acts as an insulator, and its varying quality as such depends largely on its water content. The relatively temperate climate which we enjoy for our latitude is influenced to a considerable extent by the humidity of the atmosphere; were it much less on average, we should experience greater extremes of heat and cold.

From the angler's point of view, humidity is the key factor which regulates the amount of heat which the water of the river can gain from the sunshine and atmosphere, or lose to the air. In this, evaporation plays a most important role and, as mentioned earlier, the loss of heat at the surface of the water which evaporation causes often determines whether or not the chain of events which brings about a taking time can occur. Consequently our assessment of how the degree of humidity fits in with the other circumstances is an essential task.

One extremely important aspect of evaporation is that as the air warms up it becomes capable of absorbing a greater amount of water. The result is that when weather conditions have brought about a suitable rise in the temperature of the water without interference from evaporation, evaporation may then begin to operate so as to prevent a further increase in water temperature which would increase the accessibility of oxygen beyond the level suited to a taking time. Thus evaporation maintains oxygen accessibility within the bracket which produces sport. This favourable influence on the pattern of taking periods will be discussed later.

Fortunately, visual evidence of the state of the humidity of the atmosphere is plentiful. Some aspects of it have long been recognised by anglers as reliable indications of the prospects of sport, whether or not their full significance has been appreciated.

The "soft" light, regarded as being so encouraging, is, in fact, an excellent sign that the degree of humidity is satisfactory. The thoroughly disliked "hard" light shows that the air is too dry.

References to "a nice, soft, morning" cover both the temperature and the humidity, and therefore, in accordance with popular belief, there is then even better promise of sport than merely when the light is satisfactory.

Many descriptions are given to the surface of the water when it has a glassy appearance. Most of them are very apt and all are given in disapproval. It is usually the result of the combination of relatively low humidity, high atmospheric pressure, and layers of thin cloud at a high altitude. I think it is just as bad when the water looks a beautiful blue, which is brought about by the same conditions but without the cloud in layers.

In case the novice should have a wrong impression, it should be pointed out that whether the light is hard or soft it has no direct bearing on the mood of the fish. The light can be soft on a sunny day and hard when it is overcast. It is true that the salmon can be dazzled; sunshine straight down a pool is almost impossible to contend with successfully, but this is purely a local aspect. If other conditions are suitable for the fish to be on the take, it is only necessary to find lies at a different angle to the light for response to be forthcoming.

On calm days it is a comparatively simple matter to judge whether the balance of the sunshine, the warmth of the air, and the degree of humidity will bring about a rise in the water temperature. But wind can cause some difficulty, because it brings with it several subsidiary problems.

Only in rather unusual cases does the tendency of the wind to increase the aeration of the water require our attention, and those are confined to periods of drought or extremely hot weather when the actual amount of dissolved oxygen in the water may be becoming too low. Ordinarily the oxygen content will be satisfactory and its availability will not usually be affected seriously by an increase in the amount caused by aeration. But the physical disturbance of the water by the wind can be an important factor in an entirely different way. It will be appreciated that when a taking period is in progress it is necessary for the angler to create a suitable illusion before he can expect an offer from a fish, and a strong wind often makes this very difficult, much more so than many anglers believe.* When the season has advanced to the point when the salmon show little or no interest in sunk-fly or downstream spinning with large baits, and when fishing near the surface has become most profitable, then, especially, almost every angler will have had the experience of hooking a fish during the briefest possible lull in a period of strong wind. It is pretty obvious that when the wind drops momentarily there cannot be any instantaneous change as far as the fish are concerned, apart from the appearance of the surface of the water and the background to the lure which is being offered to them. Therefore I believe that the correct level of availability of oxygen keeps the salmon in a responsive mood despite strong wind. The only problem then is to present the fly suitably. Lulls in the wind permit this, and I think it is sound policy to search for the most sheltered lies.

Apart from the preceding two aspects, wind does nothing more than modify or accentuate the influence of the other weather factors; it can, therefore, be helpful or harmful according to the circumstances. When the air is dry, for example, any wind will facilitate evaporation, which can be fatal to prospects in spring by making the water colder, but is often helpful in summer by making the water cooler. The most notable favourable result of wind is when, in the late spring, it retards slightly the start of a taking period, but prevents the temperature of the water rising too high in the early afternoon. Thus it cuts out the gap in sport and produces the longest period of good fishing we are likely to have throughout the season.

One must be on guard not to be deceived by the wind,

* See Commentary B.

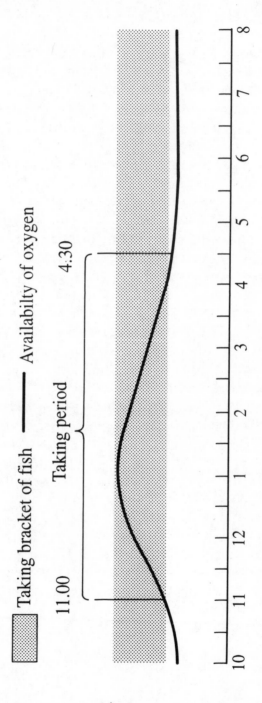

Diagram 1. Taking-time pattern for an ideal, spring-like day in March.

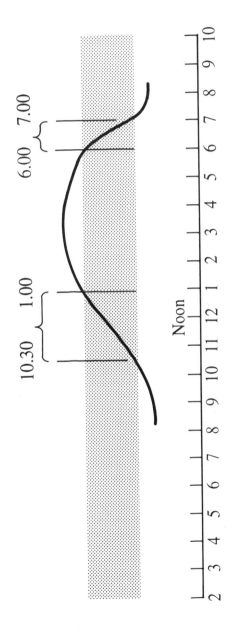

Diagram 2. A calm, sunny, cloudless day in April.
Note the rapid decline of oxygen availability in the early evening.

especially in early spring. A suitably humid westerly can feel very chilly and give the impression that it will do no good, but it is practically certain to be appreciably warmer than the water, and therefore is well capable of producing very good sport.

The famous "soft" westerly will never fail to be recognised, of course, and perhaps it would be pleasanter not to mention the dreaded cold dry east wind. But it should be remembered that the direction of the wind does not matter in the least on the normal type of tributary-fed river. It is quite possible, particularly on a local basis, to have a wind coming apparently from the wrong quarter but which is of the quality that will make for good fishing.

One particular set of circumstances which it is often very rewarding to watch carefully is when the amount of humidity and warmth in the atmosphere does not appear to fall far short of requirements, but there is a light wind which is just enough to swing the balance and keep the fish in an unresponsive mood. If the wind is from any other source than the Atlantic, it will probably die away in the evening and then, in a very short time, the water can warm up that fraction needed to bring the fish well on to the take.

The direction of the wind is a most involved problem in the case of short rivers which are composed of the overflow water from large lochs or lakes. Such rivers require separate study, because the circulation set up by the wind on sheets of still water determines whether the outflow consists of surface water which has been exposed to the atmosphere or comes from the under-currents which are usually much colder. Consequently a change in the direction of the wind can cause sudden changes in the temperature of the river which do not seem to tie up at all with the nature of the atmosphere at the time. It must be known, therefore, how the contours of the surrounding land deflect the winds from the different quarters, whether the loch is deep or has a large surface area in relation to its volume, and if in any particular circumstances the current from any large tributary is enabled to maintain itself right up to the outflow.

It is essential to have all possible local advice to gain useful understanding of such rivers without long personal experience of them; but there is one feature which is common to most of them, and the appreciation of it can be immediately helpful. The fish tend to use such rivers more or less as very large-scale salmon ladders. They wait in the estuary until conditions are right and then they can make the journey to the loch in one trip, with only a few short pauses for rest. Many of them never become residents in the pools. Consequently, knowledge of the regular resting places is of vital importance.

In certain rivers of this type some of the salmon are native to the stretch below the loch and remain there, while others return to spawning grounds in tributaries beyond the still water. When such is the case, the observing of running fish is the most reliable indication of conditions which will probably induce a responsive mood on the part of any salmon which are resident in the pools.

The popularity of worm fishing in most rivers of this sort speaks for itself.

Returning to the main subject of general factors, the barometer is about the only guide to prospects one can get before the journey to the fishing commences, but it is the trend of change which should be noted rather than the actual reading. Tending downwards is usually associated with favourable conditions, while rising pressure is less promising. Once beside the river and able to assess all the features of the weather and water, the atmospheric pressure can be taken into account seriously. Medium to low is only likely to be unfavourable in hot weather, when it may lead to too high an accessibility of oxygen. High pressure should not prevent sport if all other influences are quite favourable, but it is a serious hindrance if the atmosphere is drier or colder than one would wish.

Cloud need only be dealt with separately on a tactical basis close to or during a taking period. If an abundance or lack of cloud is the principal feature of the weather, thereby affecting the amount of sunshine, it will automatically be taken into account in assessing whether or not the temperature of the water will rise. As the time approaches when sport is anticipated, changes in the amount of cloud should be noted. In cool conditions increased cloud will probably cause a little delay, or even cause a gap in sport if it has begun; whereas in hot weather the arrival of heavy cloud, especially when it is pushing a cool breeze in front of it, will expedite the awaited taking period in the evening.

At times when the prospects of sport are generally good, however, cloud is likely to be so variable that it will not be a vital influence one way or the other, and only major changes should cause any concern.

It need hardly be said that in very changeable weather one cannot anticipate the pattern of sport for the whole day, and it is necessary to be an opportunist. A good appreciation of the chief factors, though, is then at a greater premium than in the more idyllic conditions when salmon fishing seems to be rather too easy – that is, in the eyes of any others than salmon fishers.

Taking-time patterns

The fact that changes in the temperature of the water always lag behind those of the air plays a major part in forming the patterns of taking times.

In addition, in settled weather the cumulative effect of the heat of the day makes the decline of the temperature from the hottest point much slower than was the rise to it. For practically the whole of the salmon season, consequently, the periods of sport to be had after midday are far longer than those in the forenoon. The many popular sayings which show approval of "a fish on the bank before lunch" are evidence of the general recognition of this.

The splendid sport which is so often to be had in the evenings is due to the combination of the slow decline of the temperature of the water and its reducing rate of decline as the day wears on. This holds the availability of oxygen in the proximity of the bracket of suitability for the fish's activity for long periods, and any little beneficial influence, such as the dropping of the breeze or the gathering of cloud to hold the heat in, is sufficient to extend the period of sport almost indefinitely.

The advantages of this fortunate aspect of the trend of the availability of oxygen can be seen in most of the diagrams of taking times, such as Numbers 1 to 4, but it shows to the best advantage in the late spring when sport often continues until it is quite dark. Even as early as March, however, there can be many days when fish are taken at dusk.

The closing phase of the day also offers an excellent opportunity of sport in apparently very different circumstances, but nevertheless due to the same basic reasons. At various times of the season when there has been a spell of fairly wet weather and the river is running boldly, but not in spate, and overhead conditions are very favourable for good fishing, it is often found that practically all the salmon are moving up the river and sport is very scarce. It does not seem like a proper run of salmon, and is perhaps a case of an opportunity being too good to miss to make minor, leisurely adjustments. However, it is very exasperating, because one feels that one ought to be catching fish, but nothing happens. On such days, almost invariably, the fish stop running at the edge of dusk and are then certain takers. If the exact time is known when the light will begin to fail, it is possible to predict almost to the minute when a fish will be hooked.

Grilse especially are very subject to behaviour of that sort, which is perhaps the reason why on many rivers they are regarded as being much more difficult to catch than salmon.

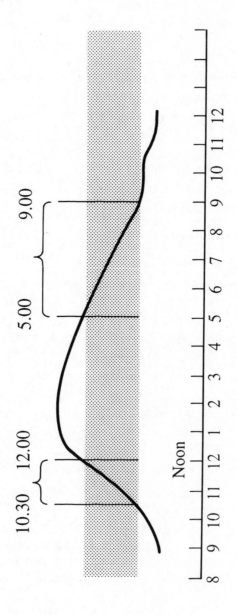

Diagram 3. A typical, seasonable day in late May or early June.

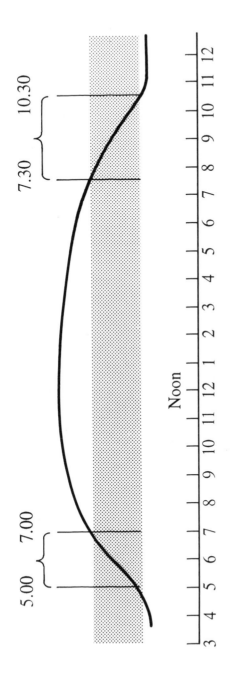

Diagram 4. A pattern commonly experienced during "high-summer" conditions.

41

At times a shoal of grilse can be seen moving slowly upstream in "follow your leader" fashion, and almost every one will show in practically the same place as its predecessor. It is very easy when fishing a run to be deceived into thinking that the same fish is being seen time after time, and that it should be possible in some way or other to get an offer from him. But if the fish are definitely on the move, it is extremely unlikely that one will be caught until close on dusk unless an established resting place is tried. On some of the smaller rivers it is possible to wait at such lies until a fish is seen to halt there, and then be pretty certain to get him within a few casts. Only a small proportion stop to rest, though, because the leisurely, almost playful way in which the grilse proceed up the river in those circumstances is no strain on them.

On a day which has been good enough to suggest promise of a long evening's sport the sky is the best guide as to whether it will materialise. Almost complete coverage with large layers of light grey cloud is perhaps the best, but a cloudless sky usually results in an abrupt end to sport at a comparatively early hour. This is often followed, just before dusk, by mist gathering in the fields and the river "steaming". The quick drop in the temperature due to the escape upwards of the heat causes condensation and makes the water in the atmosphere at ground and water level visible, and one can be sure that the availability of oxygen fell below the bracket of the fish some considerable time earlier – more precisely, when the fish went off the take.

A similar phenomenon resulting from a quick drop in the temperature happens during the morning when a very light cold breeze sets up following a warm cloudy night. The mist high on the hillsides can be seen to be rolling quickly downwards, and, as is commonly known, this is a certain sign that the fish will be extremely stiff.

There are occasions on hot, close summer evenings when the availability of oxygen remains too high for the salmon until the daylight is finished; but that gives the opportunity of the exciting experience of playing a salmon, perhaps a large one, in very shallow water in the dark. Up to dusk, the salmon lie quietly in the deeper, slacker parts of the pool to avoid an excessive intake of oxygen, and then suddenly the surface of the water becomes alive with swirling fish and long furrows advancing swiftly to the neck of the pool and into the rapid water beyond. I believe that that is the result of the aquatic vegetation commencing to give off carbon-dioxide. In order to avoid a concentration of it, most of the fish then seek the fast, well-aerated water, while some drop down the pool to the swift flow of the glide at the tail. With the overcast sky which is usually associated with those conditions, it goes extremely dark quickly; but the fish, in their newly chosen lies, respond well to a large low-water fly. A salmon taken in the inky blackness is a very thrilling conclusion to an otherwise hopeless day.

According to the height of the water, the lack of sport on a hot summer's day can be due to too great an availability of oxygen, or an insufficiency owing to the dissolved oxygen content of the water having got too low to satisfy the fish despite its easy accessibility. The latter case is usually confined to times of drought, and the fish then try to stay in the rapids where the current is the heaviest, or if they are untenantable, in the glides if they are deep enough. Blustery, showery weather is then needed to bring about any chances of sport quickly. When the availability is too great and the fish are sheltering in the deep water, the rising of a good breeze will often bring them on to the take very quickly indeed. Swirls of fish near the surface are the sign to try backing-up or stripping, and this accounts for many a salmon when the runs and streams will yield nothing. If the blow continues and seems to be doing its job well, a careful watch should be kept on the lies in the current. If the fish are seen to be gradually returning to them, they are fairly certain to be takers.

Almost every season, at some stage or another, a pattern of taking periods develops which is considerably different from what is regarded as standard for the time of the year, and persists for several days until it is accepted as normal. Then there is a tendency to put too much faith in those hours and neglect other parts of the day. It should never be difficult to ascertain the reasons for such periods of sport, and then not only will it not be disappointing when they finally cease to recur; but, also, the taking times which will replace them should easily be anticipated.

The remarks, in the same vein, with which I will end this section may seem to be unnecessary if the reader happens to be in agreement with me; but I have to say that several very experienced salmon-fishers who now accept broadly the oxygen theory are reluctant to believe that the salmon do not form habits. I maintain that every day is a new day to the salmon, and what happened yesterday has gone forever. The period of the salmon's response, if any, will be strictly in accordance with the availability of oxygen as influenced by the weather and water factors; whatever occurred previously will not matter. The salmon have no calendar excepting, if you like, the movement of the sun in the sky. If April conditions suddenly assert themselves in July, one must act accordingly immediately and not cling to the idea that the pattern of taking periods will only undergo a relatively slow change because the salmon have got into a groove, so to speak. Similarly, I believe that the river experience of the salmon between taking times, and during previous periods of response, has no influence whatever on its involuntary reactions when it comes on to the take afresh. It is as if it had awakened from a long unbroken sleep since leaving the sea. If a correct illusion of a suitable prey for the circumstances is created the salmon will take it, although it may have seen an identical lure dozens of times before – fished correctly, but not at the right time. Experience proves that one July day salmon will take a No. 5 low-water Blue Charm at noon, when for some time earlier the only daylight response has been to the smallest sizes in the very early morning and late evening.

The opponents of this view, who argue that the difficulty in catching stale fish compared with fresh-run ones is because river experience makes the fish too wise, should remember what a nuisance red fish can be in autumn when one has set one's heart on catching one of the beautiful clean fish which then make their appearance in some rivers.

Seasonal factors

The depths of winter are still with us during the opening days of the season in January, and it is not surprising that the discomfort which we suffer in snowy and icy conditions gives many anglers the impression that the salmon will feel similarly. This, of course, is far from the truth; the most certain prospect of sport at that time of the year, I should say, is when the river is fringed with ice and heavy snow showers are being blown on a westerly breeze.

Perhaps the two hours or so of sport which is to be had, commencing close on noon, is as much as most of us would want; but in that spell three or four magnificent springers can well be taken. That does not leave much time for doleful thoughts about the weather.

The reader will have deduced that the reason for favouring such conditions is that the ice is a reliable indication that the water has been very cold overnight, while heavy snow showers ensure that the temperature of the atmosphere is relatively warm. This will almost certainly produce the very slight improvement in the water temperature that is needed in those circumstances to put the salmon into a taking mood.

Contrasting with that situation, when a bright, cheery sort of day supersedes cloudy, miserable-looking weather, the probability will be that the air will then be colder than the water. In that case the chances of a fish will be rather remote. At the same time, although there is no doubt that a rising tendency in the temperature of the water is necessary for a reasonable period of consistently good sport, I do not join those who say categorically that salmon cannot be caught when the air is colder than the water. With the water in this low range of temperatures, and the salmon so recently arrived from the sea, the availability of oxygen is never far from the level required for response; a result is that some other factors peculiar to this situation may sometimes produce very brief opportunities of sport. I think that the changing of the trend of the density of the water a little before it approaches freezing point perhaps has a beneficial influence on the oxygen accessibility, but I regret that I have not had sufficient experience of weather and water combinations of this sort to provide the basis for a decided opinion. As a general rule, however, when, at this time of the year, there seems to be no hope of the atmosphere being capable of raising the temperature of the water, the angler who does not put up his rod will not miss much.

It will probably be a long spell to go from icy to thundery conditions, but between them everything should be fairly straightforward in the assessment of prospects of sport. It is difficult to discover whether the static electricity in the atmosphere prior to a storm is a deterrent to sport in its own right, because, usually, the build-up to lightning occurs when the normal factors which have to be considered are all against the promotion of a taking period. Often sport is to be had very soon after the storm has passed; but again it will be found that the trends of the changes in the temperature, humidity, and pressure of the atmosphere are such as to give good reason to expect the fish to start taking, regardless of there having been a storm. Consequently, whether or not the fish react unfavourably to thundery conditions, it is sufficient for us to regard them as simple evidence that the normal factors are very unpromising. It should be remembered, of course, that the state of the atmosphere which is usually associated with thunder-storms is of the kind that takes the availability of oxygen too high; then a downward trend in the temperature, and reduced humidity, are the chief requirements to bring the availability down to the level acceptable to the fish.

The next problem to be met is likely to be excessive acidity of the water. After there has been some hot weather in the late spring or summer, spates in most salmon rivers are subject to a phase when the water is lingy or peat-stained.* Unfortunately this usually happens when the river is running in nicely and is at the best fishing level. Then, although perhaps an odd fish is taken here and there, sport is never good; but at the same time some salmon will usually be seen to be running. I think that the explanation of this rather peculiar and seemingly contradictory situation is that the main concentration of acidity is low down in the water where the settled fish are lying, and there the availability of oxygen is unsuitable. The runners seem to confine themselves to thin water farther away from the main stream than in a springtime spate, and any fish caught are usually taken from shallow resting places. All this suggests that the top layers of the water are freer from acidity and provide greater availability of oxygen. The examination of a moorland pool after heavy rain in summer shows distinctly how the deep stain, and presumably greatest acidity, sinks towards the bottom and leaves the surface of the water relatively clear. It seems to take the deeper, more slowly running pools quite a long time to recover after the period of excessive acidity; during the few days after the river has cleared, the faster runs and streams are the most productive.

Plenty of bright sunshine appears to be a help in dispelling

* See Commentary C.

excessive acidity, and, in autumn, a frosty night seems to do a lot of good in this respect.

Subsidiary indications

The state of the atmosphere and its influence on the general circumstances of the day are reflected in innumerable ways. Some are so simple and commonplace that, in the ordinary approach to salmon fishing, without any thought of the availability of oxygen to the fish, it would probably seem incredible that their meaning could be of any value at all.

Now, I should think, the reader will feel that most of these matters are so obvious that they do not require to be mentioned, and such a reaction would be very pleasing to me. But, for the sake of the record, I will cover a small selection of these signs. They have been chosen on the grounds of their requiring no effort to be observed – it would be indeed difficult to fail to notice them – and the sequence is convenient.

Let us then make a trip to the river, and, as we can please ourselves on this sort of journey, we will have everything as we should most like to see it. All instruments will be ignored, including the barometer.

When we pass through the gate into the field our principal appreciation of the weather has already been made. We were glad to see the dome-like appearance of the sky, making our little part of the world seem cosier and more intimate, and not overlooked by the distant mountains. We noted the softness of the sunshine, light and breeze: we were satisfied that everything was most promising. To check up on the question of evaporation, we had watched the road surface and were pleased to see that it was quite damp under the overhanging trees, and not altogether dry elsewhere. Now we note as further confirmation of the favourable degree of humidity that the grass is quite wet.

The river looks particularly friendly, with no glare on the

water, and, despite the ripple and the disturbance of the current, we can just make out the vague forms of the larger boulders on the bottom.

At nine-thirty on a mid-April morning, nothing could be better. The salmon should be on the move relatively early and we tackle up without any waste of time. Quite soon we see a few wagtails fluttering among the pebbles at the water's-edge. That is splendid! They know there will be a hatch of fly and they are ready and waiting; and that is a far more positive guide than any instrument readings could possibly be.

Although it is still perhaps a little early to start fishing, and we are reasonably confident that we have not missed anything so far, we have no intention of doing so. We begin casting. We know that the line is in perfect order, but we can see that it is not going to be easy to keep it floating well for very long. This, however, does not displease us. We remember that those days when we are able to cast so well that we don't resent spectators and the line floats as if it would do so for ever, seldom produce much dividend for this apparently good performance.

We now notice some activity of parr in the tail of the pool. The wagtails have started making their little hovering trips over the water, and at any second we should see some of the duns that have started to hatch. But having got this marvellous reassurance that the temperature of the water is lifting, and that the availability of oxygen should be about right for us to be able to expect some offers, we are more interested to watch for something other than the flies, delicately pretty and graceful though they are. Yes – there it goes! A beautiful head-and-tail rise – the true taking kind. We have a wonderful chance to be into a fish any time now.

Presently, having had proof of the responsiveness of the fish, a splendid salmon safely beached, we fear that sport might quieten off in the early afternoon. We look at the sky.

The sunshine is quite strong, the clouds are more broken and, now, white instead of their earlier greyish-whiteness. It is getting warmer although the breeze is a little more lively, and we see that the grass is drying. Evaporation has started, and we judge that the atmospheric pressure has begun to increase. By keeping the water temperature down, in spite of the warmth, this should hold water conditions to our liking through the middle of the day. If this trend continues there will be a very abrupt end to sport in the late afternoon when the air cools down quickly; but we shall certainly have no complaints. On the other hand, if our luck holds, and the breeze subsides and the clouds gather again, preventing too great a loss of temperature and humidity, it should be a good evening too. But that will be uncertain for a few hours and we shall have to wait and see.

Working on the oxygen theory, that would be just about a perfect day. It would be interesting to know what percentage of anglers who rely on their normal experience would rate it so.

Let us now look at some of the points more fully. Few anglers under-estimate the value of a head-and-tail rise. It is almost a certainty that the fish is a taker, and it is a reliable indication that others not showing will also be responsive. There is the possibility, though, that some who have had disappointing experiences will not share this confidence in the head-and-tailer. I will try to dispel any doubts.

Sometimes fish are to be seen to show in a somewhat similar manner, though very infrequently compared with the number of genuine head-and-tailers. But the length of time during which they break the surface of the water is considerably greater, and the tail action suggests that they go down again much less steeply. Usually this happens in the evening in smooth water, and the fish tend to move upstream between rises. If a close watch is kept it will be seen that the open mouth breaks the surface of the water, and the movement is very much like that of a goldfish in an ornamental pond excepting that, due to swimming against the current, the back and tail of the salmon show when the head goes under the surface again. Such fish seem to be getting gulps of air, and if my observations have been correct, they do not take anything from the surface of the water. I have never been able to induce any response from fish showing in that way, and I think it is important that they should not be confused with genuine head-and-tailers.

Some of the fish that swirl just under the surface of the water, particularly near the edge of the river, are definitely takers; the offers I have had in the nearest likely lies to the positions of such rises seem to confirm this. It is quite certain, though, that not all fish that behave in that manner are doing so as a result of being in a responsive mood. If observation is kept on a number of fish jostling for a specific lie, it will be seen that the end fish which gets pushed too far away will move off at a tangent, swirl under the surface of the water as it turns downstream, and then swim round and push in between the other fish again from behind. This happens mostly when the water is very low and warm, and then no doubt there is a big premium on the best lies.

For my own part, when conditions are at all normal and prospects look reasonably good, I always work on the assumption that fish swirling under the surface are takers. But, of course, they cannot be regarded as being nearly as reliable as head-and-tailers.

Normally it is a bad sign when the fish fling themselves out of the water in any or all directions; but the occasional fish behaving like that is a welcome sight when most of the leaping is of the low, forward, business-like variety of the runners. In the spring, if a lot of salmon are moving upstream, it can be taken for granted that some of the fish are not doing so. They will be in a suitably responsive mood. It is a safe indication that a salmon which jumps haphazardly across the current is not running, and it is encouraging to have this reassurance that there are at least some residents, whether or not the leap of the particular fish is promising in itself.

On many rivers the popular preference is that no fish should show at all. I do not disagree that the best and longest taking periods often occur without any fish being visible on the surface, but for me it adds enormously to the fascination of fishing a lie when a head-and-tailer has just been seen there. There is no doubt whatever though that it is far better that no fish should be seen than that many of them should be jumping clear of the water.

On occasions the salmon in quite deep water can be seen rolling and flashing on the bottom. One popular theory is that such behaviour shows that the fish know that it is going to rain, and that there will be no sport until the river has had the freshening up that is in prospect. There may sometimes be quite a lot of truth in that idea, because before the rain clouds appear, visibility does often become extremely good and the transparency of the water becomes greatly increased. But I attach much more importance to the fact that the ability to see the fish so clearly is an indication of the approach of rain, than I do to the possibility that their rolling is a sign that they know of this and therefore are unlikely to be responsive. In the first place, it cannot be assumed that the fish in the deep water only roll when it is going to rain, because they might perhaps also do that when they cannot be seen and no rain is imminent. Secondly, I have taken fish in the evening in continued fair weather on a sufficient number of occasions following an afternoon when the fish were rolling and flashing, to be able to refute the suggestion that it is useless to fish again until after the rain.

As far as the floating of the line is concerned, high atmospheric pressure and low humidity undoubtedly are a big help, as not only does the line tend to dry each time it is in the air during a cast, but also the skin tension of the water is greater, and particularly so where the surface is fairly smooth. It always seems very ironical that when the control of the line can be achieved so well, it is hardly worth doing; but we have to accept that such is the case. When sport is good there is nearly certain to be trouble with the line. But so long as the fly can be fished fairly satisfactorily, it is better to put up with this partial sinking than to waste time trying to remedy it – which in any case would not remain effective for long. It is well worth the trouble always to have at least one duplicate reel and line ready for a quick change when it becomes essential. Nothing is lost by missing lies that necessitate the line crossing slack water, and concentrating on areas with a good overall flow that helps the line to float. It should be mentioned, of course, that in heavy, thundery conditions when the line misbehaves, that should not be regarded as being favourable, because the oxygen supply will be either too high or too low for the salmon.

The activities of the birds and the whereabouts of the flies and aquatic insects can easily be interpreted into a running commentary on the state of the atmosphere. In a bad east wind, none is to be seen. When superficially everything looks all right, but the barometer is too high and evaporation excessive, any birds feeding in the air will be seen to be flying quite high. If sport with the salmon is good, the angler will seldom find himself to be at the riverside alone, or in silence. Often the birds will be claiming their share of any duns, stone-flies or sedges, and the seagulls will join in noisily; the blackbirds, the thrushes, and other song birds will sing near by. When the riverside is deserted, the angler will usually lose nothing by leaving it so.

No doubt the naturalist, who previously may not have thought of salmon-fishing in terms of the accessibility to the fish of the dissolved oxygen in the water, will easily prepare a comprehensive and extremely useful list of all the subsidiary indications. At the same time, I hope that the scientists specialising in the related subjects will endorse the feasibility of the salmon being affected in the ways suggested, and the validity of the interpretation of the relationships between the elements.* The angler can be assured, however, that the discussion in these pages of circumstances of weather, simply seen, that lead to taking times, will be found to be reliable, whether or not I am guilty of attributing any wrong implications to them.

* See Commentary D.

Reading River Currents

The behaviour of water

Very few anglers, however skilful they might be, can escape some feeling of envy of the man who knows his river very intimately. He selects with confidence the type of water to be fished according to the prevailing conditions, and walks past unsuitable stretches without hesitation. He has the ability to judge where the rate of flow close to the bed of the river (probably contrary to appearances at the surface) is suitable for the fish in the particular circumstances; and he knows in which of the probably occupied lies the current will help him most to present his lure satisfactorily.

The stranger finds it difficult to decide where the salmon are likely to be; when he does manage to locate them, he is liable to spend too much time on lies where the current makes it extremely difficult to fish successfully. Then there is the danger of his taking the fatalistic view. Only long experience, he thinks, will provide the personal knowledge he needs. In the meantime he must simply keep on working hard and persevering until time eventually reveals the secrets of that particular river.

It is undoubtedly true that no two rivers are alike and no two pools are alike; but water does obey the same laws always, and salmon follow the dictates of the same influences everywhere. Some study of the relevant factors, therefore, should be at least helpful in deriving the full benefit from any experience on unfamiliar water.

Gravity is, of course, responsible for all the inherent flow of the river, but the effects of it are modified by other factors which deflect or transform the vertical pull into horizontal flow. These other physical factors are that water cannot be compressed, and that it will not permit the creation of a vacuum within itself, from which suction arises.

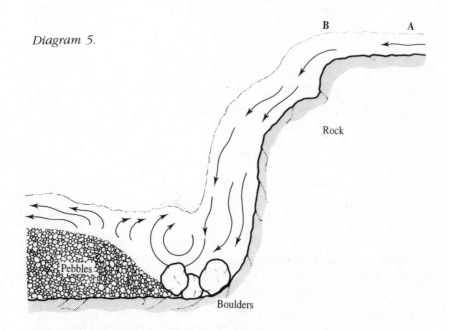

Diagram 5.

Two distinctly different types of flow result and it is most important to be able to identify them.

Firstly, when the gravitational pull can exercise itself forcefully on the water and is deflected by the slope of the river bed into horizontal or forward pressure, it is hardly possible in natural conditions for it to occur smoothly and evenly. Backwashes in all planes from horizontal to vertical are set up, and quickly, if not altogether, the forward flow becomes concentrated in the level near and on the surface. The movement of this layer is resisted by the pockets of slack and swirling water beneath it. Unless some additional impetus is given to the forward pressure by a further drop in the bed of the river, it is quickly divested of its power, and the movement is reduced to no more than that required to equalise the level of the surface.

Secondly, the flow caused by suction results in a fairly even speed throughout the depth of the water, and is not subject to haphazard changes of direction nor any diminution of its momentum.

All this is easily appreciated by considering what happens at a waterfall. In diagram No. 5, the current at A is very fast. But that is not due to the immediate gravitational pull at that point, because there the pull is vertical and prevented from operating on the flow, other than to keep the water compact, by the flat rocky bed of the river beneath it. At point B the force of gravity is able to assert itself and the water drops, and, as it will not allow the formation of a vacuum, suction draws the water from A to replace it.

The impetus of the falling water is largely lost when it reaches the bottom of the falls, much like a stone dropping to the ground, and what little remains is deflected in all sorts of directions. In the falls-pool the water has no inherent forward pressure to make it flow away. Consequently, a slight dome of water tends to collect, but gravity will not allow this to build up. The strong vertical pull on this extra surface water is deflected by the water beneath it (which cannot be compressed) into a much weaker, almost horizontal, pull which causes the top layer of water to flow gently away. The subsequent behaviour of that flow depends on the changes in the capacity and character of the channel through which it must pass until ultimately the water is again taken over by the influence of suction.

In diagram No. 6 the more inclined fall results in a gradual deflection of the movement of the water, and it loses considerably less of its impetus by impact with solid matter or other water than is so in diagram No. 5. Consequently the falls-pool does not get washed out as deeply and is more

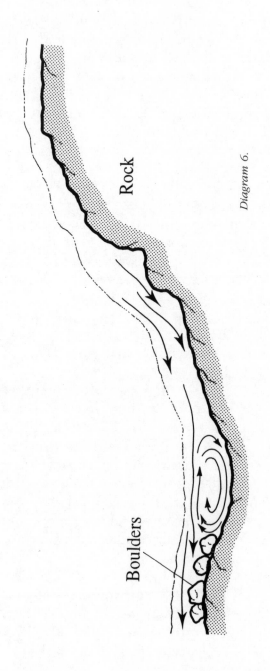

Rock

Boulders

Diagram 6.

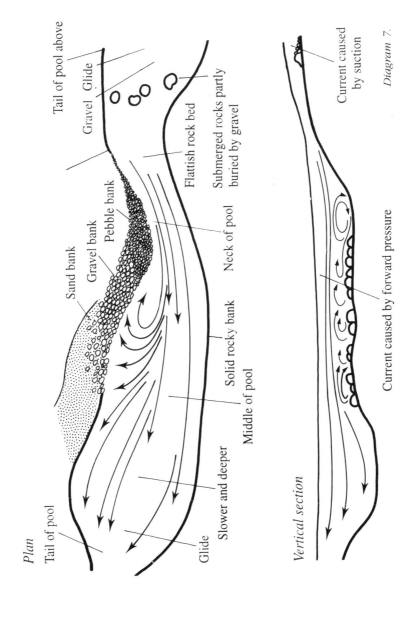

Plan

Tail of pool above

Gravel Glide

Flattish rock bed

Submerged rocks partly
buried by gravel

Sand bank

Gravel bank

Pebble bank

Neck of pool

Solid rocky bank

Middle of pool

Tail of pool

Glide

Slower and deeper

Vertical section

Current caused
by suction

Current caused by forward pressure

Diagram 7.

59

elongated. Nevertheless, the backwashes and undercurrents still arise, and the residual forward pressure is compelled to exert itself mainly on the surface layers.

Diagram No. 7 shows the plan and vertical section of an average sort of pool that is to be found on many rivers. It includes all the same features as the waterfalls, but everything is elongated; the head is a rapid rather than an actual fall. Pools which are less well defined than in diagram No. 7 are simply the same thing over again, but elongated still further, and the proportionate size of the component sections can vary infinitely.

On the larger rivers and the lower reaches of the medium-sized rivers, the longest of pools still behave similarly, but there are often pools within the pools, so to speak. These minor pools only show faintly on the surface of the water (unless the river gets extremely low), but the variations in the flow of the water are similar to those in the obvious pool.

The man with adequate experience of the river exploits these minor pools without any waste of time, while the stranger has to fish carefully over many times as much water to be sure of covering the spots that matter. A little careful observation should save much of that.

The steadier middle sections which are a feature on some pools, and which on the larger ones are subject to containing the minor pools, tend to have a fairly even flow between the surface and the bottom layer. This bottom layer is usually much slower owing to the resistance and turbulence caused by the irregularities of the bed of the river.

It will now be seen that water drawn forward by suction is the only type which is not subject to the surface speed being appreciably faster than the lower levels, where the fish usually lie.

As was mentioned earlier, no two pools are alike and the variations are infinite. But, however they occur, the same features of the bed of the river and its edges or banks always have the same influence on the current. It is entirely wrong to think that any river can have any special peculiarities of its own as far as the behaviour of the current is concerned.

Glides, runs and streams

The distinctly different characteristics shown by each of these three types of water lead to their being regarded by some anglers as features of the river which are additional to the pools. But they cannot be separate entities; they are always integral parts of a pool. It is very misleading to think of them otherwise, because that would add much pointless complication to the problem of currents.

Deriving its flow from suction as it does, a full scale, or river-wide glide must always be the tail of a pool, and the converse is also true, whether or not it is of fishable depth. This can be a little confusing when the glide covers the whole of the middle of a pool and, apparently, extends right up to a very short head which may be barely discernible. Nevertheless, it must still be treated in all respects as a glide, because the particular way in which suction influences the flow of the water is evident in varying degrees throughout its length.

The regular even flow of the glide, being practically as fast at the bed of the river as it is at the surface, removes all bulky obstructions excepting rigid rocks and boulders, which cause little resistance in relation to their mass. The current will not permit the establishment of extensive pockets of slack or steady water, and any remaining obstacles to the flow cause a minimum of turbulence, which is quickly dispelled. The mark which an obstruction causes on the otherwise smooth surface of the glide does not spread outwards, but narrows down and is very localised. Any number of obstacles cannot in any way impede the flow, because the suction will not be denied. If rocks compel the water to go through a narrow channel, the speed of the current accelerates so that a sufficient volume of water passes that point to satisfy the demands of the suction.

Glides are extremely difficult to fish with greased-line. There are no little irregularities in the current to help to hold the fly so that it can be led or checked across steadily. Unless there is a very helpful breeze, the pressure of the water forces the fly to the surface where it skims rapidly to the side. If the difficulties can be overcome by using a double iron or weighted fly, sport in the smooth water is particularly enjoyable, because at least the bulge of practically every fish that takes is seen and quite often the salmon's tail breaks the surface.

Of all classes of water the run is probably the most highly favoured by both the fish and the fisherman. Its flow being that of forward pressure, it is most commonly found at the neck of a pool, but it can extend to almost the whole length of a pool from the head to a very short tail. When the rate of fall of the river is small, the forward pressure from the head of the pool expends itself very quickly; the rough-looking or popply neck is short and usually followed by a very steady section in the middle of the pool. In areas where the river negotiates a fairly good regular slope in the land and does not cut a gorge for itself, the runs can be of quite great length. This is due to the fact that after the flow of water leaves the head of the pool, it gets additional impetus here and there from further slight drops in the bed.

The speed of the current in a run varies considerably from place to place, and one lie or another is almost certain to suit the fish at any time of the season. The very uneven, bustling nature of the current helps the angler to make the fly behave almost exactly as he wishes, and the fish have such good cover that nobody needs to mind very much if another rod has preceded him down the run.

The number of boulders on the bed of the river has a big influence on the extent of the areas of turbulence beside which the fish lie; but even when the bottom is composed

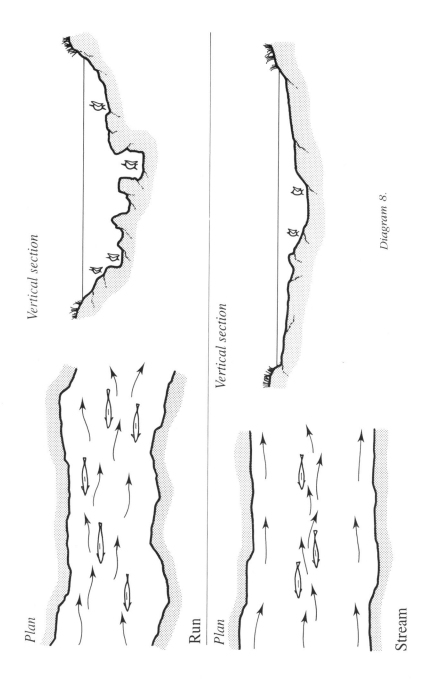

Vertical section

Vertical section

Plan

Run

Plan

Stream

Diagram 8.

chiefly of pebbles, the extra speed on the surface caused by the forward pressure results in underwater swirls. The fish have no difficulty in finding comfortable pockets of suitable flow which meet their requirements admirably.

It often happens that in the wide, steady area in the middle of a big pool there is a sudden narrow drop in the bed, perhaps under one bank; the current speeds up so that it is the beginning of a run which, sooner or later, peters out again. The flow above and adjacent to the run is more smooth and inclined towards the run. In a big water this feature would be undiscernible, but if the river fell to a low level, the shallower water above and alongside the run would come under the influence of suction to feed the faster flow. It would then be seen that the area had become a separate small pool, with a little rapid at the head of the run. (In other words, and this would apply to the whole river, the lower the level of the water, the more the contours of the bed of the river express themselves on the surface; the higher the water, the less are the individual features of the bottom able to exert their influence up to the surface level.)

Such a situation is what was referred to earlier as a minor pool within another pool. From this it will be appreciated that while from a practical point of view a run can be other than the neck of a pool, it is nevertheless always created by the same basic features of the bed of the river, and its behaviour is always such as to be extremely attractive for fishing when the volume of water is adequate.

The word stream is used so commonly in a general sense to imply current or flow – in conversation I am as guilty as anybody – that it would be helpful if there were some other name by which to identify the class of water so known. However, good streams are so delightful to fish, and the name fits so well, that I am content to risk the possibility of confusion.

Where the stream has enough depth here and there to provide lies for the fish, the behaviour of the current is

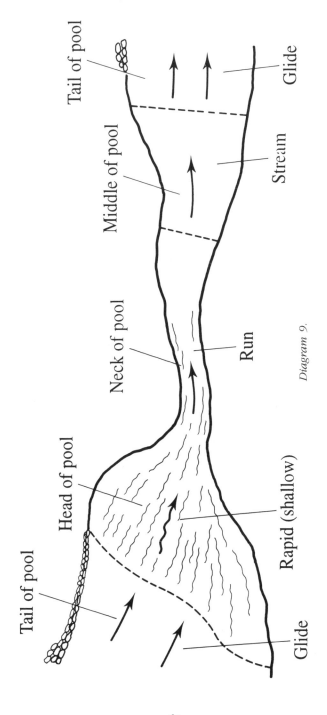

Tail of pool

Glide

Middle of pool

Stream

Neck of pool

Run

Head of pool

Tail of pool

Rapid (shallow)

Glide

Diagram 9.

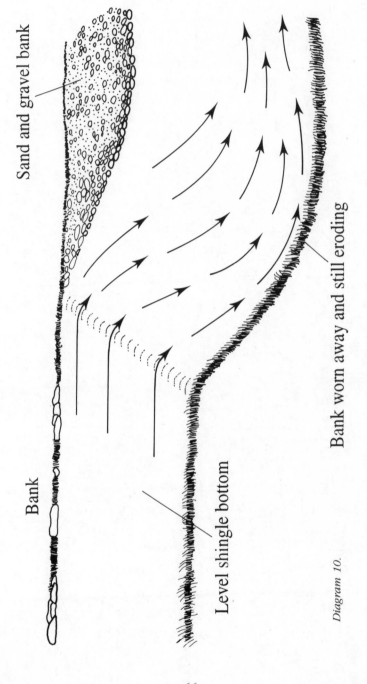

Sand and gravel bank

Bank

Level shingle bottom

Bank worn away and still eroding

Diagram 10.

relatively the same as in a run. But a stream fishes even more easily than a run, often without the necessity for any mending whatever. When the fish are taking in such water, they seem to do so more freely than anywhere else. Unfortunately, good productive streams are more rare on the majority of rivers than any other class of water, and the level of the river has to be just right for each individual stream to be worthwhile. Therefore streams are not nearly so generally important to anglers as the runs and glides.

A stream can, of course, narrow into a run, and a run can widen into a stream, but it is rather a mistake to regard a stream as simply a shallow run. A typical run can contain lies distributed haphazardly from one edge of the current to the other, as shown in diagram No. 8, whereas the ideal stream has a main channel, not necessarily situated centrally, in which most of the lies are found. It is the fact that the speed of the current gradually diminishes from the main channel to the side that assists in covering the lies adequately without much mending.

Unlike runs, too, streams are subject to containing miniature glide and rapid combinations. These are very noticeable and attractive, but are quite tricky to fish with normal tackle and long casts, owing to the variation in the speed of the current which the line traverses just outside of the tiny glide. This causes too much check, and therefore drag, on the fly for it to fish the lie below effectively. However, such lies are usually only of real interest if the weather is warm and the river low, and then a single-handed rod and short line are adequate and overcome the difficulty. If a long line must be used, a large mend straight upstream when the fly is in the glide, and then a steady lift of the rod, will usually ensure the covering of the lie at a suitable speed.

It will be appreciated that these small glides and rapids

are parts of further examples of minor pools within large ones. It is a help towards fishing them to full advantage to make observations of the whole of their influence within the stream, because immediately above the glide there is often a further good lie which can easily escape notice.

An extremely important aspect of the value of a true appreciation of the difference in the nature of the flow in a glide on the one hand, and in a run or stream on the other, is realised when the planting or removal of boulders is contemplated with a view to the improvement of a particular stretch. It will be seen that the removal of obstacles reduces the speed of flow in a glide and facilitates it in a run or stream; the planting of boulders increases the speed in a glide and impedes it in a run or stream.

Sometimes obstructions are constructed to cause the washing out of a deeper place suitable for a lie. This works well in a stream if it is so arranged that the water flows over the obstacle at an accelerated rate, thus forming the start of a little rapid. But it is useless to attempt it in a glide because the urgent demands of the suction do not allow the water any liberty to depart from the most direct line to the point where it is required.

The ability to differentiate between the types of current also removes any doubt about the demarcation line between pools. Anglers are frequently heard to refer to what is actually the head of one pool as the tail of the pool above, which can be very confusing. The reader will now agree that the head of the pool starts where the drop in the bed of the river, or the increased rate of slope downwards, commences to give the water the impetus of forward pressure, thus forming a rapid (which may be quite shallow), and at the same time creating the suction which draws the water forward from the area above.

On a broad shallow, the line dividing the glide and the head of the pool below is clearly marked by the little white

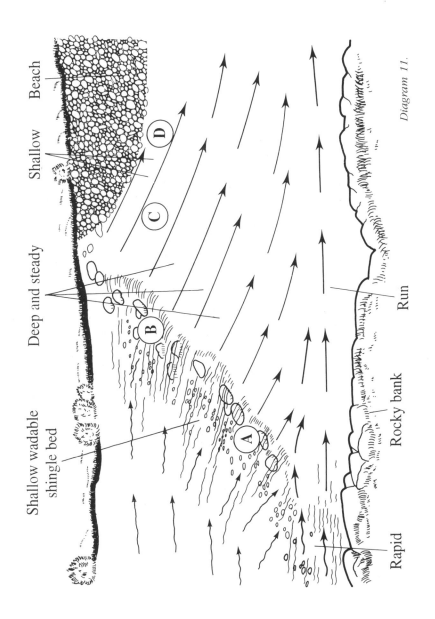

Beach

Shallow

Deep and steady

Shallow wadable
shingle bed

D

C

B

A

Run

Rocky bank

Rapid

Diagram 11.

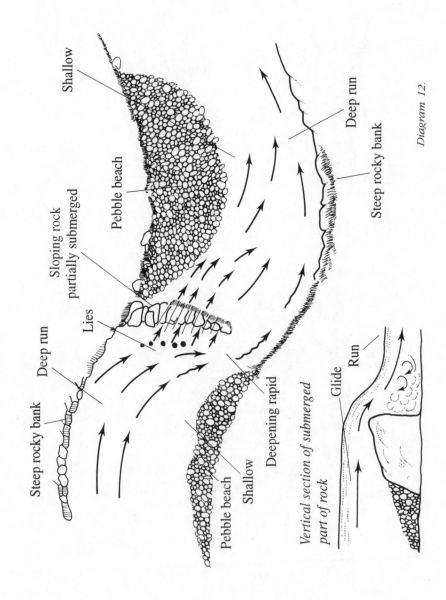

Shallow

Deep run

Pebble beach

Steep rocky bank

Sloping rock
partially submerged

Diagram 12.

Lies

Deep run

Steep rocky bank

Pebble beach   Shallow

Deepening rapid

Glide

Run

*Vertical section of submerged
part of rock*

plumes of water where it begins to break. Diagram No. 9 shows such a place.

Use of current

Intimate knowledge of the river gives a mental picture of all worth while casts, and it enables one to put the line down at the correct angle to fish well with the first throw. The stranger will probably have to cover the pool several times before he becomes familiar with the variations he must employ to get the fly to work satisfactorily; but a few minutes' careful observation should cut out a lot of unnecessary fatigue and, also, greatly improve the chances of getting offers.

The highest priority in one's memory of a pool should be given to the casts where the fly will fish well all the way round without much mending. A good introduction to the kind of situation which makes this possible is to be had from the study of an artificially constructed dam. In diagram No. 10, the bed of the pool above the dam is level shingle, and the flow is parallel to the straight banks until it approaches the lip of the dam. The water falls vertically and the suction draws the water over the top of the dam by the quickest route, which is at right-angles. The water all along the bottom of the fall has to get away and, as no part of it can compress any other part of it, the only course open is to flow forward at right-angles to the dam. This causes erosion of the right bank, but the resistance of the bank to the force of the water diverts some of the pressure downwards, and this washes out a deeper place beside the worn bank. On the left bank spates deposit sand and gravel in the slack water, which has no scouring action, and when the river returns to normal the top of the sand bank is left exposed.

It will be seen that to wade in a little way from the sand on the left bank, and cast along the line of the flow, would enable the fly to be held at the dangle indefinitely. This means, of course, that the fly can be fished as quickly or slowly as is desired by casting more squarely or less so across the current, which makes for the ideal fishing position.

Covering the pool from the right bank, where wading would be impossible, is not an easy proposition as far as the lies in the middle of the river are concerned, because very long casts at an acute angle to the current and much mending are needed to prevent the fly from crossing the current too quickly.

Natural divisions between two pools roughly similar to the construction in diagram No. 10, are quite common, and many of them have practically the same flow as shown in diagram No. 11. This run is just as easy to fish as the previous one; but, due no doubt to the apparent vantage point gained by wading, and the habit of always starting in at the top of a pool, this type of place is frequently fished in such a way that a valuable part of the run is entirely wasted. There seems to be a strong urge to wade out to A, cast at forty-five degrees to the bank, and continue so doing through B and C to D. Anglers who fish thus will say that although they see a lot of fish at the top of the run and all the way down, they rarely get an offer until they are fishing from the vicinity of D, and there it requires a long throw to reach the fish. From this they assume that the salmon seen higher up are not in good taking lies.

It will be understood immediately that from any point from A to C, the forty-five-degrees cast will drop the fly in the run, but the line is then held straight by the flow between the rod and the run, and only the end crossing the run can pivot round. Consequently, the fly skims round quickly and is then held at the dangle very near the surface on the edge of the run. It is not surprising that such a performance kills very few salmon.

The way to take full advantage of this favourable combination of currents is to wade to a position several yards short of A and cast almost squarely towards the other bank, thus crossing the flow between the rod and the run at about forty-five-degrees. That allows the line which is clear of the run to float round gently in the right direction, and this checks the fly in the run just about the right amount without any further help from the angler. If, however, it is thought that the fly is being checked too hard, the rod can be held high at the completion of the cast and then dropped slowly, at the same time allowing a big loop of line to run out from the hand as desired. In that way a good deal more water can be covered very effectively with each throw. This is a very easy and pleasant manoeuvre which is very rewarding wherever the current will hold the line out towards the run and allow the line to be drawn forward by the stronger flow of the run. Similar casts should be made all the way through to D, and great satisfaction is to be had from using the current to do such good work.

Underwater obstructions often cause similar outward flows of water towards the main current, and these can be employed in the same way. The break on the surface showing this state of affairs may not be very obvious, and care is needed to seek it out. In this connection it cannot be stressed too strongly that the minor contours of the surface of the water are much more easy to detect when looking upstream than downstream. Viewing the water from below is vastly more revealing.

Another particular construction of the end of one pool and the start of another is worth detailed study because of its peculiar attraction for the fish. On many rivers it is extremely rare, but occurs quite frequently in gorges and in areas where the river traverses rock strata.

Diagram No. 12 shows a long sloping outcrop of rock protruding across the river to a point where it is buried by gravel. But for the rock, this stretch would be a deep, fast run swinging from one side of the river to the other. There is a heavy rapid in the space between the rock and the other bank, but a good volume of water flows over the edge of the

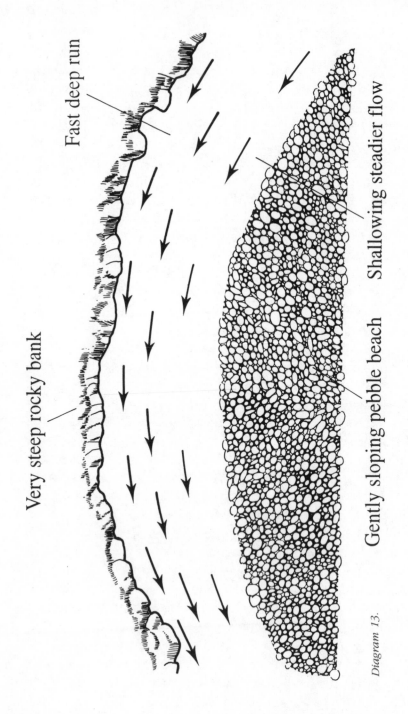

Fast deep run

Shallowing steadier flow

Very steep rocky bank

Gently sloping pebble beach

Diagram 13.

rock and falls to the lower level at the other side, with the result that suction draws surface water from the run and at an oblique angle to the main direction of the current. This results in an underwater area, between the gliding surface layer and the lower current that conforms to the run, in which, judging by the way the salmon favour such a position, the state of the pressure provides a suitable lie. It is extremely difficult to fish from either bank, and weighted flies and much mending are essential; but the fish show beautifully when they take, and it is well worth the trouble of mastering the technique of presenting the fly correctly. Ordinary low-water flies are practically useless, and a heavy line performs much more satisfactorily in cases of this sort than a light one.

These are, of course, summer lies, and as it is frequently found that the occupants are responsive when sport cannot be got in the normal runs, the reasonable assumption seems to be that the division of the current provides a particularly desirable resting place for running fish. Anglers who are familiar with lies of this sort value them more than any others for summer fishing.

The types of currents and lies mentioned are only a fraction of those which it could be interesting to study. As with most other activities, however, the successful handling of one problem seems to make the next one easier. If the angler is equipped to go to one unknown and rather peculiar pool and fish it fairly satisfactorily through having made an adequate assessment of the current, he will get pleasure, not irritation, from any new complexities of current which have to be solved.*

Changing levels of the river

Some pools fish well at all reasonable levels; others are only at their best at specific heights of water. It is an annoying

* See Commentary E.

waste of time to take a long walk to a stretch of which one has high hopes, only to find that the current does not behave as was expected, and that there is no chance of sport. The experience needed to provide a reliable mental picture of many pools in all water conditions cannot be had quickly; but there is a very useful substitute.

When fishing any pool which is interesting enough to attract one there again, note should be made of any important features of the banks, beaches, rock formations, which will start or cease to affect the current at a different level of the river. For example, a large obstruction which is clear of the current will be an important factor when, with the river rising, it starts influencing the flow. When fishing a nice run from an innocent-looking sandy or silty shallow area, it should be remembered that, in a high water, it will probably be covered by a large patch of slack water which will make it difficult to fish the lies well, or perhaps even to reach them.

The construction of a pool which is almost certain not to undergo a basic change of character when carrying a bigger volume of water, can be perceived at a glance. The inside of a gentle bend is the easiest example, as shown in diagram No. 13. The deep run gets much faster as the river rises, and then the salmon move over towards the inside of the bend. But for fishing purposes the current remains just as helpful at all but extreme levels. This is a class of water more generally useful perhaps than any other.

In these days of intensive drainage in the uplands; of bare hillsides that were once wooded; of riverside constructional work; on many rivers the violence of floods is greatly intensified. It is resulting in the greatly accelerating mass movement of pebbles and gravel. A pool with lovely runs and streams at the end of one season can be a useless shallow flat at the beginning of the next. All pools do not suffer equally badly, thank goodness; but there is a great tendency towards change. Unless the angler has a satisfactory understanding of currents, much time is lost before he becomes familiar with the new situations. There is always so much more to learn about fish, fishing techniques, the river itself, that he is an extremely fortunate man who does not need to be always taking time for observation. It is when conditions are obviously useless for fishing, or when there is certain to be a long wait before sport can be expected, that time can be so well and interestingly spent in study of the river. No matter how familiar the stretch is, it is seldom that there is not something to be seen in a new light; apparently quite minor points can later prove to be invaluable. What is perhaps as important to me as anything is that the more closely and eagerly I watch a salmon river, the more its beauty is revealed to me.

Where salmon lie

A good salmon river is essentially fast flowing; a layman's impression would probably be that the fish revelled in the rapid and rough water. Many novices begin their careers with this idea firmly established. Their suspicion is aroused when they are told that the idea needs drastic modification.

The fundamental behaviour of salmon in fresh water is based on economy of effort. Their purpose is to spawn. But though their survival proves that they are adequately prepared for this, their instinct says that nothing should be risked which could endanger the maintenance of their strength to fulfil that single duty. Consequently, there is nothing to support the idea that play could be an intended part of their river life.

No doubt some movement is needed to help the shedding of bodily wastes which must occur despite the fact that they do not eat and digest food in fresh water. But they often lie motionless for very long periods, only broken by spells of activity during taking times, or when, perhaps, they are irritated by parasites, and it seems that that is sufficient exercise to maintain their health.

All that salmon require of the current of the river, before spawning, is to provide lies where the flow of water supplies the right amount of oxygen with no work for them, and to help them to travel upstream with the expenditure of only the minimum of energy.

In many parts of the current there are places where the speed of flow changes considerably in the space of a few inches laterally. By inserting itself between two different strengths of current, the salmon can borrow force from the faster flow to hold itself effortlessly stationary against the weaker one. Similarly it can gain help to move upstream.

In this respect the observation of moving fish is more impressive than that of resting ones. Some of the bridges from which running salmon can be watched have extensive shallows immediately above them. Towards the end of the spate, when the water is neither coloured nor deep, the progress of the fish can be followed for a hundred yards or more. When two or three salmon go up one by one at very short intervals, it could be thought that they were simply following the leader. But soon afterwards an individual fish unhesitatingly picks the identical route, making the same minor changes of direction, the same relatively sudden turn towards the bank. Then it is realised that there must be positive physical reasons for the choice of course. When a big number of individual travellers, with no other fish in sight at the time, have been seen to take exactly the same path, no doubt can remain that it has been specifically selected. There can be only one reason for this: it is, obviously, that the salmon are equipped to sense instantly the line of division of speeds of current which they can use most advantageously.

Where regular lies are to be seen on flat rock, salmon stay in that identical spot so long that the stone gets worn free of the fine mossy growth that is present all around. A fish taken from such a place often has a sore patch on the forward part of the belly, where it has been rubbed. Such lies never remain vacant long at a suitable time of year and height of water. Precisely the same position is chosen when the new tenant settles down to motionless rest. It is quite clear that the combination of current and the shape of body of the fish results in a very convenient balance. I do not think that the touching of the rock by the fish is a necessary factor in the maintenance of position. In my opinion the salmon keeps contact with the rigid material so that, while dozing, any loss of position through slight change in current will be registered and can be rectified immediately.*

From this it can safely be assumed that fish which are seen to be lying still in a run or stream are not sheltering in the slack or swirling water behind an obstruction. That would be quite unsuitable both for effortless retention of position and for intake of oxygen. They are using the influence of the turbulent area on the flow alongside the obstruction to produce the divisions of speeds of current which suit them. Consequently, parts of pools composed chiefly of surging backwaters which keep shifting the line of the forward flowing water to one side and back again, do not provide lies. As all anglers agree, they are not worth fishing.

In a run or stream, while it is not possible to translate the surface of the water into *precise* indications of suitable lies beneath, it is easy to see where the flow will *probably* provide the necessary requirements at one point or another in the vicinity. Without previous experience of the stretch, it can be judged which parts should be covered with particular care.

It should also be appreciated that the division between a relatively slow and still more slow speed of current can do the same work for the salmon as that between a fast and less fast flow. This enables the fish to find lies to suit their

* See Commentary F.

oxygen requirements at any time of the season in normal conditions.

The foregoing suggests the explanation of the fact that the main bodies of glides are not favoured by salmon. The points where suitable variations in the speed of the current are available are normally in the areas where the glides begin, or along the sides where protruding rocks create little bays of still water, or when a subsidiary side-rapid draws a secondary glide away from the main one.

The difference in the behaviour in glides and in runs of the water within bays that are created by protrusions of the bank is, of course, further evidence of the opposite characteristics of the two types of flow. The forward impetus in a run disperses itself in any direction where the resistance to it is insufficient to hold it back, thus forming a backwash. In a glide, suction is supreme and will not allow any diversion of the current from the direct route to its source. The result is that the pull on the water which it cannot capture from behind an obstruction is very even all around; and, therefore, it remains relatively very still.

If the salmon are seen during the daytime to be in the main body of a glide, it is a pretty certain indication that the content of dissolved oxygen in the water is becoming too low. The salmon are being compelled to maintain their position laboriously in the fastest suitable flow they can find to satisfy their oxygen needs.

In that case there is no hope that the maximum possible improvement in oxygen accessibility will increase the amount available to the fish to the level required to bring them on to the take.

On dusk in warm weather when the salmon have been sheltering from an excess of oxygen in the deep water, some of them will go into the main body of a suitable glide for a spell; then the chances of sport are excellent.

In the wide tail of a pool where the glide converges on to a narrow rapid, parr by day and seatrout by night have a

The River Lune at Newton, showing Ingleborough in the distance. The demarcation line can be seen between two pools, running diagonally across the river. The glide (the tail of the upper pool) breaks into the rapid (the head of the lower pool).

The River Lune at Rigmaden. The head and neck of the Kingfisher pool. The water in the foreground is the beginning of a splendid run.

The Aberdeenshire Dee. A fine example of a stream in a pool.

A typical spring salmon from the Aberdeenshire Dee.

High up the Aberdeenshire Dee, between Braemar and the Linn of Dee.

The River Feugh, a tributary of the Aberdeenshire Dee.
Note the aeration that takes place.

A rock-bound stretch of the upper Lune.

Righyni at a River Board spawning station.

Association water on the River Lune at Underley. In the mid distance a typical run can be seen under the far bank and opposite the extensive pebble beach.

Fishing the greased line on the Hampshire Avon at Somerley. Polaroid glasses help to watch the line.

Bernard Venables on hand to gaff a Hampshire Avon salmon for the author. Here the fish is tiring. Earlier it had been "walked-up" about forty yards away from the danger of the broken water and dense aquatic vegetation adjoining the bottom of the glide in the foreground.

The River Muick, a tributary of the Aberdeenshire Dee. In summer this is inclined to be peaty and acid and can spoil the fishing in the vicinity of its confluence with the main river.

The River Tweed near Kelso. The water being fished is quite a perfect example of a stream.

greater quantity of the most easily visible food floated over them than in any other place in the river. They do not have to worry about conserving their energy; it is constantly being replenished. Obviously such places offer a very profitable exchange for them. That such parts of the river are the most impossible for the salmon to live in puts into relief that the problem of the salmon is unique.

Tributaries and confluences

When data is available from a good number of rods covering several beats on the same river in reasonably favourable conditions, a uniform picture of the periods of sport is usually revealed – as would be expected. Often there is agreement as to practically the precise times when response commenced and came to an end.

But sometimes the reports appear to be conflicting. An analysis shows that there were two, or sometimes three, distinctly different patterns of taking times.

Such situations can nearly always be attributed to the joining with the river of a major tributary, and to the difference in the qualities of the water in the respective flows.

It might be thought that the influence of the smaller source of water would be unimportant, restricted to a very short stretch below the confluence. That, however, is seldom the case; evidence to the contrary is not difficult to find.

When a valley is closely flanked by steep hills, spates in the tributaries often reach the main river before the latter begins to rise. Then the segregation of the two sorts of water can be seen distinctly; in some places it continues for a surprisingly long distance downstream. It is most interesting to see how the coloured water of the tributary claims its share of the river's course, widening out over shallows and contracting again where the channel narrows. Even through most of the runs and rapids, there is very little tendency for the two flows to mix with each other. The type of pool which is most likely, ultimately, to cause a general compounding of the water is where large rocks below a heavy rapid result in deep billowing backwaters and confused irregularity in the location of the main current.

Of course much depends on the construction of the bed of the river where the tributary enters. But usually erosion and the disposition of boulders and pebble-banks (caused by the force of the converging or, at one time, conflicting currents) result in there being very little tendency for the waters of the river and the tributary to mix at the point where they first make contact with each other.

It follows that when such a large tributary is not in spate, and there is no visible difference between the two flows, they will still behave in a similar manner. Each will occupy its correct position relative to its proportion of the total volume. In other words, the main river and the major tributary do not join together in homogeneous unity – they meet and flow side by side until some dominating feature of the bed of the river causes haphazard divisions of the current resulting in the two different sorts of water being blended together.

On a wide river that can be fished from both banks simultaneously, therefore, it will be seen how that characteristic in the vicinity of a confluence can result in three different states of water – that of the unaffected part of the river above and opposite the tributary; that of the tributary; and that one farther downstream composed of the blend of the former two.

The temperature, the content of dissolved oxygen, and the degree of acidity of the tributary almost invariably differ very much from those of the main river. That accounts for the variations in sport.

It is often extremely difficult to judge whether the stretch dominated by the tributary will be affected beneficially or harmfully with regard to short-term response from the fish. It is advisable for the stranger to avail himself of any reliable local advice.

Usually the tributaries will be well aerated and partly spring-fed, thus resulting in the content of dissolved oxygen being very good. But sometimes, as when they drain small tarns or lochs, the acidity becomes the predominant factor. Then the influence of the tributary tends to be harmful to the prospects of sport.

Some such tributaries which are chiefly composed of the over-flow from still water appear to be fairly neutral in their effect on fishing when conditions are calm and normal, because then the flow is of genuine *surface* water from the loch. But, with the wind in a particular direction, the volume of water from the loch into the tributary is increased, and then the water becomes much more acid. Sport then is very likely to be scarce in the affected areas. Such a situation can usually easily be detected by the discoloration of the water. The pools which suffer most can be avoided.

In early spring it occasionally happens that excellent sport with greased-line is being enjoyed on long stretches of a river above a confluence; but below it, on the same side, response is indifferent or even very poor. It is fairly certain in such cases that it will be found that the tributary is several degrees colder than the main river above or by the opposite bank. Then sunk-line or spinning might prove to be an adequate answer; but it is also possible at that time of the year that the area affected by the tributary will remain poorly stocked for a while.

Later, however, when the river has warmed up a few degrees, there can be an almost entire reversal of the position. If there is then a greater availability of oxygen in the area influenced by the tributary, as will often be the case, it may be particularly favoured by the salmon. The taking times will be different from other stretches in the locality, and sport will probably be considerably better than elsewhere. If the river gets rather low the fish cling tenaciously to such lies. Then it is the effects of a tributary of that sort which are usually the explanation for any accumulation of a large number of salmon in a confined space.

Perhaps the most peculiar situation which can arise from the entry of a tributary, and is least likely to be suspected of coming from such a cause, is when a good run of salmon in early spring stocks all the pools up to a certain point in the river. Beyond that not a solitary fish seems to venture. There are places where, almost every season, this happens sooner or later at practically the same spot. The reason is usually sought in the immediate vicinity. The possibility that it could be caused by a tributary, say two or three miles higher up, is not even considered.

But if the halting of the fish is too abrupt to be explained by the possibility of their having simply no desire to go farther, and there is nothing else apparently responsible – such as natural or artificially created stretches of unsuitable water which would be too big a strain to negotiate – it is most probable that a tributary is the cause. Sometimes, it seems, the blend of the tributary water with that of the river must be adequate for the salmon's requirements; but either sort undiluted by the other is unsuitable for them to continue their journey in the prevailing conditions.

On strange water it would not be possible, on the basis of one's individual fishing experience, to make a quick and accurate appreciation of all the probabilities concerning a stretch of river containing a confluence of any importance. But the angler who has a permanent interest in such a beat should soon be able to establish the extent to which the tributary maintains its separate identity, and locate the first pool below the entry of the tributary where the water is of reasonably even quality from bank to bank. Soon the picture of how the salmon favour or avoid any of the three different classes of water will build up. Before long, the indications noted so far, and the knowledge of the influence of the availability of oxygen on the behaviour of the fish, enable a fairly reliable view to be formulated of the probable trends as the season advances. Each added item of useful data improves the angler's chance of making a correct assessment of what will be the most profitable stretch upon which to concentrate on any particular occasion. Eventually he will understand his beat so well that, without hesitation, he will know where the best sport is available at all times. And, what will not be an unimportant matter as far as most salmon-fishers are concerned, he will have the satisfaction of knowing why the peculiarities and varying potentials of the different pools are such as they are.

Greased-Line Fly Selection

Policy

The pleasantness of greased-line fishing tends to over-shadow the fact that it is extremely effective and versatile. The wide variety of waters for which it is suitable, and the very long part of the year during which that is so, justify its being regarded as the most important method of fishing for salmon.

Had the possibilities of greased-line fishing been much less, the experience of the sixty years or so since it was introduced would probably have established more definite limitations to the types, patterns, and sizes of the flies which could be used successfully. As it is, the flow of new or modified ideas shows that the fly for greased-line fishing is still in a very active state of evolution – and, perhaps, a relatively early stage.

Any system for working out the pattern and size of fly for a particular occasion must, therefore, be able to allow for all the existing varieties, and for new developments which will surely come from time to time.

It also seems to be essential that the method should be comprehensive enough to be able to reconcile the apparently contradictory situations which so often occur. Very small flies and large ones may be successful at the same time; dark flies and very light ones are taken in apparently the same circumstances. If the system can provide an explanation, not only should that give a guide to the possibly successful alternatives, but it will also refute the suggestion so often heard that the fly does not really matter much, that the only serious factor is whether or not the fish are on the take.

Colour and form

Let us ignore our own point of view, and think only in term of what the salmon will see of the attempt to produce a suitable illusion. We will divide all flies into four main and two subsidiary groups on a tonal and functional basis:

1. SILHOUETTE.
2. TRANSLUCENT ILLUSION.
3. NORMAL IMAGE.
4. FLASHING ILLUSION.
5. TRANSLUCENT ILLUSION/NORMAL IMAGE.
6. NORMAL IMAGE/SILHOUETTE.

The salmon being monocular for the major part of its field of vision and incapable of varying the amount of light which is permitted to enter the eye, it is very subject to being dazzled, frequently in one eye only, but often in both. That greatly assists the fly in achieving the necessary illusion. But, of course, the fly must not fail to be seen, nor must it be seen so clearly that it loses its power of deception.

In this the background to the fly is obviously important. In our first consideration of the categories of colour and form, we will assume the nature of the background, and study it in detail later.

1. Silhouette.

When the sun or source of strong light is at such an angle that neither eye of the salmon can escape dazzle entirely, colour in the fly near the surface cannot be appreciated. In those circumstances the background to the fly is usually bright, and, therefore, the fish has no chance of seeing anything but the silhouette, whatever the colour of the fly. Consequently there is no point in using anything other than a black or extremely dark fly. Hackle movement is of no importance and a relatively bulky fly is usually an advantage; very slender dressings could still perhaps escape notice, especially in fast water.

The Silhouette Fly offers the best opportunity for experiments in size and form. With the colour factor eliminated, any preference which is shown by the fish must necessarily relate only to the length and proportions of the fly.

2. Translucent Illusion.

If a light of dazzling strength is at an oblique angle to the river, the vision of only one of the salmon's eyes will be affected seriously; and although the background to the fly will still probably be bright, there will be a danger that the Silhouette Fly will look too stark and unlifelike to create a suitable illusion. In that case the Translucent Illusion offers the best prospects. The dressings are not of course fully translucent, and that is not necessary. A fly with a silver or very light-coloured body, and stiff pale-toned hair or hackle, permits sufficient light to pass through it to make the outline indefinite. The body is best kept as slender as possible, with the main bulk of the fly provided by the hair or hackle; that should be strong enough to resist any tendency of the water to close it on to the body. Hackle movement, therefore, is unwanted.

The aim should be for the fly to have a slight tendency to glow, and the inclusion of a little fluorescent material can be helpful. It will be seen that although any density of colour is to be avoided, the Translucent Illusion gives good scope for trying different shades of colour.

When the direction of the light favours the use of the Translucent Illusion, there will usually be variations in the angle of the current which can produce lies where neither eye of the fish escapes dazzle. In such cases the Silhouette would be the effective fly. Consequently, whenever the Translucent Illusion appears to be the correct fly and actually accounts for fish, the Silhouette may also be successful here and there. It is well worth using for the second time down the pool.

It might be thought that when one eye only is dazzled, the fish will move to a fly seen only by that eye, and that could be the reason for the Silhouette being taken. I cannot substantiate my opinion fully, but I think that when one eye has much better vision than the other, the less affected eye has a predominant influence on the fish, the dazzled one only giving warning in case of danger. For that reason I always prefer to be on the side of the pool from which I am facing the light so that the cast is fished out in the view of the more effective eye; but that eye, nevertheless, is having to contend with much stronger light than that for which it was presumably designed.

The fact that the Silhouette is often useful when the Translucent Illusion is the more obvious choice does not, however, apply in reverse. When the sun is high in the sky and the Silhouette is required, the difference in the angles at which the fish are lying does not prevent both eyes being dazzled. The Translucent Illusion would have little chance of being seen sufficiently well to create an attractive illusion.

In very fast water there are occasions when, although the Translucent Illusion is theoretically the correct fly, it does not seem to make enough impact to produce response. Then the compromise between the Translucent Illusion and the Normal Image will usually satisfy requirements.

3. Normal Image.

Dull weather and a background free from glare gives the best daytime vision that the salmon can enjoy during its sojourn in the river. Colour in the water has a somewhat similar effect. Then it can appreciate colour or tone to the maximum. The dull (when wet) browns, yellows, reds, with perhaps a very discreet use of a little fluorescent or similarly penetrating colour, are seen sufficiently well; but they are not seen too clearly to spoil the illusion, because of the tendency of the fly to match, or blend with, the background. Both the Silhouette and the Translucent Illusion would then run the risk of being seen too distinctly.

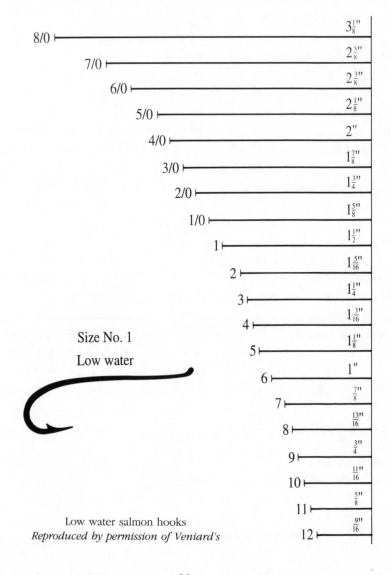

Size No. 1

Low water

Low water salmon hooks
Reproduced by permission of Veniard's

With the Normal Image fly, hackle movement is at its greatest premium. And, in view of the fact that hardly ever is one colour only relied upon, and a blend is customary, the movement is perhaps more important than any specific colour. Bulk is perhaps a matter for personal preference. I like the large sizes to be slender, and the small ones to be nymph-like in shape; but big blobby flies often account for plenty of fish and no doubt the illusion is of some sort of crustacean.

When the light is extremely poor, or the colour of the water tending to be rather heavy, the Normal Image/Silhouette will probably prove better than the ordinary Normal Image. There are many very suitable black-bodied flies, and as these will perform tolerably well also as Silhouette Flies, they are extremely useful. But an important point will be seen here. When the circumstances call for a Normal Image, there is a common tendency to go rather too far and to put on a black-bodied fly straightaway. At the same time, when the current is rather fast it is very reasonable to err on the side of the Normal Image/Silhouette.

4. Flashing Illusion.

I regard this rather as a desperation class of fly; but there is no denying that it does account for a lot of fish. When the river is low, and particularly if the light is rather strong, it is often necessary to lead the fly much more quickly than the current will carry it; it is then the Flashing Illusion is taken – presumably as a small injured fish. The silver or gold body, with a touch of red and, preferably, with a very dark hackle, will be taken when moving at a remarkably fast speed at which hackle movement is at an entire discount. What bulk is required will be achieved by tying the fly as slimly as can be done. If the flow of water is adequate, this class of fly fishes very well at the dangle – especially when it can be led round to the edge of a backwater, and then back

91

into the current again. Unfortunately, seatrout and parr are very intrigued by this manoeuvre, and one gets many false alarms. Furthermore, it has to be done on a tight line, and the takes are so sudden that it is extremely difficult to drop the rod and give line quickly enough.

Background.

The importance of the nature of the background to the fly from the salmon's point of view, and the need for the angler to visualise it reasonably accurately, cannot be overstressed. The novice will be well advised to acquaint himself with the relevant facts. It is necessary to recall the laws of light concerning reflection and refraction, and their effect on the appearance to the fish of the surface of the water beyond its "window".

When the fly in smooth water is within the cone of approximately eighty degrees above the salmon's head, the background is composed of the sky and any intervening objects above water level. Beyond the cone the smooth surface acts as a mirror and reflects a picture of the bed of the river. This precise situation happens rarely on the river, of course. Normally the water being fished will have some surface irregularities caused by the current, and probably some ripple or roughness due to the wind. The different angles of the surface in the crests and troughs, in relation to the eye of the salmon, result in the background being a distorted reflection of the bottom, blended with glimpses of the sky, hills, trees and banks. When there is any strong light, an overall sprinkling of glints of dazzling brightness is superimposed. Consequently, the background can vary from a large sombre area with a relatively bright centre patch, to a shimmering, animated mixture of colours and light. The salmon has no defence against this except to seek the shelter of a shaded area if it is available. But it cannot do that at the expense of suitable availability of oxygen, and, therefore, the fact that it will remain in a lie which is exposed to a dazzling background when shelter is apparently within reach, does not necessarily mean that it would not prefer less brightness. But, as it is inevitable that the salmon will frequently have to endure periods of dazzling conditions, it seems reasonable to assume that nature provides that this is not the cause of any great discomfort to it. In any case, that cannot alter the problem of background as far as its seeing the fly is concerned; the correct assessment of the appearance of the background is a vital factor in deciding the category of fly that should be used.

Bearing in mind that the salmon only has to make a slight pivoting movement of its body in relation to the position of its head to give it a practically complete dome of visibility extending 360 degrees round it in the horizontal plane, its impression of the daylight and the background to any object near the surface of the water is probably much more highly illuminated than our eyes would casually tend to suggest. I think it is always a wise plan to assume that there will be an under-estimate of the brightness confronting the salmon unless the evidence to the contrary is very pronounced.

Size and weight of fly

Though it would be futile to suggest that this is not a difficult and complicated problem, the easy way out – selecting a small fly that is practically certain not to err on the big side – ignores several important factors. It imposes difficulties and restrictions on the angler that he should avoid having added to those with which already he must necessarily have to contend.

I think that it will be agreed that the aim should be to discover, for several very practical reasons, the largest size that the fish will willingly take. A large fly will fish well on a stronger cast than a small one, and will usually get a better hook-hold; then the fish can be landed without any unnecessary waste of precious time during a taking period. This is not an unsporting attitude. The strongest tackle that can be used successfully with the greased-line will not permit any skull-dragging, but will help the reasonably quick playing of a fish – and that simply amounts to efficient salmon-fishing. There is no virtue whatever in taking three times longer than necessary on a fish with a cast which is finer than the occasion demands. Next, the pools can be covered effectively much more quickly with a good-sized fly than with one which is much smaller than it needs to be. The result is that if the stock of salmon is not good, there is a far better prospect of what fish there are getting the chance to see the fly while they are in the responsive mood. Not the least important point is that the killing of a fish on a smaller fly gives no assurance that it will be noticed at all, or seen soon enough to be taken by fish in other lies, especially where the current is fast and the light strong. (By now, of course, the novice who might previously have imagined that poor light favours big flies and strong light calls for small ones will appreciate the fallacy of that idea.)

Although the size and weight of the fly is not an easy problem, it can be made much less difficult by the separate consideration and disposal of any factors which are capable of individual solution.

In that respect the easier is the weight of the fly. With the variety of types now available, it is possible, within reason, to get a fly of any size which will be of a suitable weight to fish well on an even keel in any speed of water. For example, an extremely small lead tube-fly will fish satisfactorily in water as fast as is likely to hold salmon, while very large plastic tubeflies will fish round correctly and as slowly as is desired in water where there is hardly any flow at all. Consequently the weight of the fly can now be relegated to the level of functional requirement whatever the size of the fly. It is no longer necessary to select a larger or smaller fly than is thought best simply because increased or reduced weight is required to make the fly behave correctly in the particular flow of water.

Before proceeding with the general factors affecting and relating to size, it must be assumed that the correct category of colour and form has been determined, because poor judgment of that can result in a wrong impression of what is the largest size that the fish will accept. For example, if conditions were such that a Normal Image on a Low Water No. 5 was killing well, it would probably be found that if a Silhouette were accepted at all, it would have to be no bigger than a No. 8.

The complications of the question of size, unfortunately, cannot be treated independently of the fishing tactics employed, but an understanding of that is a big help in solving many of the associated problems which arise. The most important feature of tactics is that the fly fished slowly over the salmon is a much more aggressive way than when it is fished more quickly. If the fly hovers for a relatively long period within taking range of the fish, its unnatural behaviour (in that as a very small creature it is succeeding in maintaining its position against the flow of the water) is accentuated. So is the fact of its intrusion within the salmon's personal province, so to speak. On those grounds alone, less size is required to attract the fish sufficiently than is so when the fly passes over more quickly. But additionally, the detail of the slow-moving fly can be seen more clearly and critically; also the speed with which it approaches the salmon must necessarily indicate to it that there is no great hurry to take the fly should it be so prompted. And that incurs the risk that by the time it must act if it is to succeed in taking, the larger fly will have lost its illusionary appearance. Those points are, I think, adequate reasons for accepting as facts that a considerably larger fly will succeed when fished round at a suitably fast speed, and that fishing slowly definitely calls for a smaller fly. Of course, the speed of the current has a big bearing on how quickly the fly should be made to cross the lie. In my opinion the ideal that one should try to achieve is that the speed of the fly should be such as to compel the salmon to obey the impulse to take without delay, though at this stage the purpose of mentioning this is simply to establish that the size of the fly and the tactics employed cannot be divorced from each other.

The best chance to determine the maximum size or length of fly that the salmon will accept is in fairly deep water with only a moderate flow. If the water is rather fast and shallow, the fish may see little more before taking than a reversed head-on view of the fly; but in deep water his angle of sight to the fly within taking range is such that his impression of it is unlikely to be much foreshortened. Consequently it is a fair assumption that the salmon's reaction is prompted by the sight of the actual size of the fly.

From that it can be seen that the largest fly that is successful in fairly deep steady water would not be too big for faster or shallower water if fished suitably quickly. The need to change to a smaller size would only arise if it were fished slowly. On the other hand, if the first fish of the day is taken in shallow water – where only a reversed head-on view of the fly might have been seen – there is no assurance that the same size of fly would be accepted if the side view were seen in the same depth, or the normal full-length view in deep water. Therefore only the size established as being right in deepish water can be regarded as a reliable general guide for the beat as a whole.

Before the best maximum size has been found, the behaviour of the fish can sometimes be an invaluable help. If a companion with polarised glasses takes up a position (as well concealed as possible of course) from which he can watch the area covered by the fly, he may see a fish move a little way up to the fly and drop back again, not getting nearer than three or four feet. That is a certain sign that the fly is too big; but it seems that it must look right to the fish before it reaches convenient taking range, because the same fish will react similarly two or three times to the same fly if it is re-offered to him. A slightly smaller fly will usually be taken boldly after such partial rises have been seen. This seems to prove that when the fly is too big to be deceptive, the salmon will not waste the energy to get a really close look at it. For that reason I have doubted for a long time the validity of the old and popular opinion that when the fish rises and misses the fly, or "comes short", it is because the size is too large and a smaller one is needed. I am now convinced that the opposite is the case. Since I started trying to use the largest fly that the fish would take, I have not knowingly had nearly as many of the rises that have missed the fly. When I have seen them, either a larger or heavier fly, according to the circumstances, has more often than not resulted in a proper take. These "misses" usually happen, or are seen to happen, in fast glides; they are undoubtedly because the fly is too close to the surface, not because it is too large. When the fish ultimately takes a bigger or heavier fly, fishing more deeply, its head and back bulge well above the surface. The tail goes high out of the water as the fish turns to go down. This makes me think that it changes its mind at the last moment about the smaller fly nearer the surface because to take it the fish would have to break the surface much more than, for some reason, it cares to do. There are, however, occasions, usually in the summer, when the fish has no such objections. It will actually take a skimming fly near the lip of a glide.

To avoid possible confusion, it should also be mentioned that sometimes a salmon will swirl past a fly which is very much too big. But then it is clearly its intention to crack the fly with its tail as it passes, as it will a spinner at times. I don't think the fly has had any illusionary attraction for the fish then; its behaviour is due to resentment. It can be of no value, therefore, as an indication of the correct size.

The remaining important part of the problem of size, the

most difficult part, is to decide the starting-off point for any
given circumstances. Once a rise has been had, or a fish
taken, a close enough approximation to the right size has
been achieved to make it fairly apparent what changes, if
any, are needed. But till then there is such a big difference,
on a seasonal basis, between the biggest and smallest of
the flies which, on one occasion, might be the largest that
the fish would take that as reliable a guide as possible is
desirable.

If any of the points systems, based on the temperature
of the water and speed of the current, have any real value,
they have not yet been appreciated enough to stop the
growing trend to rely almost exclusively on very small
sizes throughout the season. This tendency, I feel certain,
is a very great mistake. So then if any method is to appeal
enough to be given a thorough trial, perhaps to be regularly
used, it must have a more tangible explanation to justify it
than slight changes in the temperature or speed of the water
requiring fractional variations in the size of the fly.

My suggestions start by dividing the greased-line season
into two classes of conditions. The first could be called the
normal state, applying to all times when the rivers are in
reasonable fishing trim and the weather ranges from being
cool to quite warm, but not hot. That normal state, of course,
covers easily the largest part of the season. The second class
of conditions relates to true summer-like weather when it is
noticeably more than just warm and the rivers are tending
to be at a low level.

When the normal state is in force a Low Water No. 7 or its
equivalent length in other types of flies should be regarded
as the minimum size, and one should look for any reasonable
excuse to start the day with a larger fly. Usually, when sport
is at its best, a No. 5 fished not too slowly is much the best
size and the objective should always be to work up to that
dimension of fly as quickly as conditions seem to justify. The
circumstances which are not likely to permit any increase in

size above the No. 7 minimum are poor light with the river inclined to be on the low side. Stronger light and a better water level should make the No. 6 suitable as the starting size, while sufficient sunshine to cause dazzle and a bright background, and some extra water, will probably justify the mounting of the No. 5 straight away. Slight colour in the water affects the position in much the same way as poor light, but an appreciable amount of colour favours an increase in the size of the fly. There should be no hesitation in putting on a No. 4 when the river is tending big, or the light very strong, and although it looks a bit ungainly compared with the small flies which have become unduly popular, the No. 4 will account for fish when smaller sizes will get one nowhere.

In summer-like conditions, which can well occur in late spring or in autumn and are often absent in the middle months of the year, the low level of the river and the state of the availability of oxygen tend to confine the salmon to lies where the fly can only be presented so that it is seen at very close range. Then the Low Water No. 8 is usually the biggest fly that will give a good chance, and it should be the objective to use nothing smaller if circumstances look as if they will allow that. On rare occasions good sport can be had on trout-size flies, and the fish will refuse anything bigger; but such an event is usually associated with dull, close, quiet days, which seldom give rise to good taking periods. Much more often in the summer-like circumstances there will be some breeze and plenty of sunshine when the fish are moving well. Then, in open spaces, Nos. 8 and 9 are small enough, but a No. 10 will probably be required in a shaded lie.

It should not be forgotten, of course, that at all times conclusions cannot be drawn from the use of any size of fly until the fish are in a responsive mood. When a taking period starts and a fish is hooked, the novice is easily led to believe that it was the latest change of fly that did the trick. His best course of action is then to make a reappraisal of the light and background to the fly, and assess correctly just how his fly was fishing when the offer came. This should give him a clear idea of why the fly succeeded, and whether or not a further change might be advantageous.

From that time onwards, changes in the state and direction of the light should never be allowed to escape notice, because the use of the most suitable colour category of fly will accommodate a reasonable margin of error in size. The alteration required in the size of the fly to compensate for errors in the colour category can, as was mentioned earlier, be very great indeed. Finally, in order to ensure the correct performance from the fly according to its size and weight, it is essential that the cast should always be free from grease of any sort and not resistant to immersion in the water. All problems of this sort are quickly and completely removed by the application of a little fuller's-earth saturated with water. This washes off within seconds of the cast entering the water. It should be an invariable habit to use the fuller's-earth treatment before commencing to fish from a new position if the line has been off the water for more than a few minutes. Simple though it is, this can truly make the difference between good sport and none at all.

Fly design

A well-furnished fly-box looks so complete that it seems that there is little left that has not been done in the combinations of materials and colours. It could also be thought that since so many famous patterns have produced consistently good sport over the years, the problem of fly design can be considered to have been solved.

That might be an acceptable conclusion if it were known with any certainty which specific features of the killing patterns really accounted for their success; and so it might if our requirements of flies were not rapidly becoming much more exacting.

In the days, not so very long ago, when there was plenty of well-stocked water for every rod, sport was usually good enough sooner or later with one favourite pattern or another. It seemed that it was not a difficult matter to deceive the salmon when the spirit moved him. If sport were not up to expectations, the fly was the last thing to be blamed. Such was the apparent simplicity of salmon-fishing that the trout-fisher was rather scornful about the absence of any real skill, and of the "chuck and chance it" means by which the downfall of the king of fishes could be brought about.

The picture today is very different. A continuously increasing number of rods is plying an ever-reducing total mileage of salmon rivers. Also the circumstances which bring about opportunities of sport are ceaselessly becoming more contracted. That is owing to the reduction of the mean average levels of the rivers, and the way in which the deoxygenization of the reduced volume of water increases due to legalised pollution – erroneously allowed to enjoy the name of harmless effluent. The people responsible will offer to drink the stuff to prove that it is harmless; but the salmon don't want to drink it, nor do they want it to suffocate them, which a concentration of it would surely do.

All this means that what used to be good enough in the way of flies might not be so tomorrow; and certainly future generations of salmon-fishers will need considerably greater proven knowledge of the subject if they are to be successful, not frustrated.

Amateur fly-tyers can all produce results which will catch fish, and most of them can tie neat and lasting copies of the popular patterns. But their understanding of the relative merits of the vast variety of materials now available, and of their value for the reflection and refraction of light, is not likely to be enough for progressive experiment. We must look to the professionals for the lead and the positive steps forward. Their efforts in the past, both for the angler who tied his flies and the one who bought his, suggest that the challenge of new materials and reorientated approaches to the problem will produce, from time to time, exciting new developments. The sincerity of the gratitude of the angler who, thereby, is more able to have pleasure from his salmon fishing, will never be in doubt.*

* See Commentary G.

More Problems

Range of vision of the salmon

On many rivers when the water is at normal level or lower, most of the best fishable lies are in the relatively deep and steady stretches. There the intriguing question of the distance at which the salmon takes positive notice of a fly or bait is of great importance in deciding the tactics to employ.

There is evidence that although a fish will not usually move more than a few yards to take any lure, it will, when in a responsive mood, become keenly aware of the presence of even quite a small fly at a distance of twenty-five yards, or possibly more. A salmon which has been lying motionless will be seen suddenly to vibrate its tail and perhaps lift a little when a fly crosses the current at something like the range mentioned. That will be repeated perhaps three or four times as successive casts are made at reducing distances from the fish, until it apparently loses interest and shows no further reaction to subsequent appearances of the fly. When eventually it is presented within taking range, the fish ignores it. But had the salmon been offered the fly once only, within easy reach, it would probably have responded immediately. Similarly, after being rested for about ten minutes after seeing the fly several times and then refusing it, the fish would probably rise to it boldly if it were reoffered suitably at the first cast.

This suggests that the influence of the reflex action which causes the salmon's response to an illusion is only of brief duration at any one spell. But each time its recurrence is produced during a taking period, it is as irresistible as ever.

Clearly, in the conditions under consideration, the normal practice of casting at intervals of about three yards is quite unsuitable, because most of the fish in the pool will then see the fly at least half-a-dozen times before it is within their reasonable reach. The best solution seems to be to increase the space between casts to about ten yards, thus ensuring that no fish will see the fly more than twice before it is close enough to be taken. With this greater interval between casts, it is most unlikely that every fish will be covered suitably during any one time down the pool; but the water can be traversed several times in quite quick succession on that basis with good prospects of sport on each occasion. Covering the water too intensely undoubtedly reduces enormously the chances of success, and I would say that the most common fishing fault at all times in all circumstances is continuously to over-fish the lies as they are being covered at any one time.

In summer-like conditions it is sometimes found that even a head-and-tailer will refuse the fly or bait fished round in the normal way, although it is the first time that it has been shown to the fish. Yet a small fly or light-weight minnow cast as nearly as possible to the position where the rise was seen will often be taken within a second or two of its touching the water. This accentuates the point of not letting the salmon see too much of the fly. When the water is low and clear and there is no possibility of dazzle, success frequently depends on ensuring that each individual fish gets only the briefest possible sight of the fly.

A further aspect of the reaction of the salmon to a fly at a relatively big distance is that it seems certain that it is the movement that first attracts attention – not the size, shape, or colour. If a companion standing thirty yards above the lie throws some small pieces of twig on to the water, the fish will remain unmoved as they float down. But when immediately afterwards a fly is fished across the current in the normal way, the salmon will show unmistakably that it has seen it. Any movement contrary to that of inert compliance with the flow of the water is, then, of great importance. On some occasions, possibly, the recognition of the presence of the fly is due to alarm rather than appeal to the salmon's hunting instinct. However, when the fish takes the fly almost immediately it touches the water, it does not get enough time to be critical of the fly's behaviour in relation to the current. That, perhaps, is a contributory reason why that technique kills at times when ordinary working of the fly fails. But it does seem that the element of surprise is a valuable factor too.

The fact of the salmon taking the fly or bait cast directly to the point where it was seen to rise should not, of course, be regarded as being in any way unique in principle. There must be innumerable occasions in rough rocky runs when the fish rise to the momentary appearance of lures which are fishing round in the normal way, but in such circumstances that there is no chance of them being seen by the fish until fractionally before the takes. This again suggests that it is unnecessary that the fly should be shown to the salmon for any appreciable time before it can be expected to take, and should give the angler confidence that restricting the number of casts very severely in steady water is sound policy.

No doubt there lies in the foregoing the reason for the success of upstream spinning with small baits near the surface at times when the same gear used downstream is unproductive. Many of the takes occur almost immediately that the spinner touches the water, and it is obvious that the real art in this method is in the judgment of the points at which to drop the bait as the pool is negotiated.

The novice should also reflect that as the salmon can detect a small fly at a distance of twenty-five yards or so, it will not fail to notice any incautious activity on the part of the angler. The fact that the salmon apparently does not always fear the sight of a man or animal, and remains in its lie, is no assurance that it does not become preoccupied with the presence of the moving figure above water level, however harmless it may appear to be. Any such distraction will probably be at the expense of the salmon's response to the fly, a risk that should be avoided as much as possible. On many occasions the fish will most certainly be able to see the angler when he, the angler, cannot see the fish, and unhurried movement and neutrality with the background can be equally as important as actual fishing skill. In smooth water it is also just as important, of course, to pay careful attention to concealment when spinning upstream, because the fish will have quite as good a view of the bank below them as above.

Change-over from sunk-line to greased-line

The transfer of the salmon's interest, at some period in the early part of the season, from large flies and artificial baits fished very close to the bottom to small ones near the surface, is a fascinating problem. It is one of the least understood of the many peculiarities of the habits of the salmon; it poses some most interesting questions.

The popular conception that this change comes at some specific temperature of the water implies a belief that it happens rather suddenly. Also the fact that the usual instruction on fly-fishing strategy does not cater for any intermediate stage suggests that none such is thought to be of importance, or even perhaps to exist.

Had all experience led to such conclusions, and if there were no difference of opinion as to this critical temperature level, it would be easier to accept the idea of a quick changeover as the best basis for fishing policy. But the two principal schools of thought differ so widely as to the particular temperature that it is obvious that both cannot be entirely right. And the existence of this variation (after many years of trial) suggests that the premise may be at fault. It suggests that the problem is not capable of complete solution considered only in the context in which it has usually been considered – that of the temperature of the water, purely and simply.

Perhaps the most widespread of the established views is that the minimum water temperature, throughout the twenty-four hours, must be forty-eight degrees Fahrenheit for a period of two to three days before the zone of interest of the salmon shifts up towards the surface. But on some of the most famous fly-fishing rivers many expert anglers are content to make the change-over to greased-line as soon as the water temperature breaks forty-two degrees Fahrenheit during the daytime. And records show that good catches have been made with both sunk-line and greased-line at temperatures between these two readings – variously regarded as being so vital.

It cannot be disputed then that this change which takes place in the salmon's behaviour has not been proved to be sudden and complete in one go, so to speak. It is hardly conceivable that a cold-blooded creature – and one that is altogether independent, in freshwater, of any need of food – could be affected so decisively and dramatically by any specific temperature, as such, in that moderate range. (As an indication, or the cause, of other possible factors, however, the temperature obviously may be very significant. In due course it must be considered fully in that respect.)

The success of the wooden devon in recent years, as soon as the worst wintry weather at the beginning of the season is over, offers tangible and most revealing evidence of a definite transitional period. The way in which this bait is fished round on a long line at a relatively acute angle downstream – often with very little or no lead on the trace, and usually with the rod held high so that most of the line is out of the water – must result in its being carried by the current at least well clear of the bottom. There can be little doubt that the bait fishes, and is taken, according to the depth of the water and the strength of the flow, at a variety of levels, including that of mid-water. This method has won its place for that particular time in the early part of the season because it has been proved conclusively to be far more killing than the heavy spinner bumping along the bottom. The latter now goes out of favour as soon as night frosts become infrequent.

It can be accepted then that instead of the salmon transferring their interest abruptly from their eye-level to the surface area, there is an intermediate stage. Furthermore, as the chances are that the sunk-fly and the weighted bait are often a little way from the bottom when taken, and that the fly fished on greased-line is probably deeper on occasions than it is thought to be when it attracts the fish, it seems reasonable to assume that the salmon do actually respond to lures at all depths at some stage or other.

If that is so – which I believe to be the case – the problem requiring solution, for a truer appreciation of the matter, becomes threefold. First we need to know what produces in the salmon this change of preference concerning the distance from the bottom, and then, if the temperature of the water has any value as a guide, to assess its worth. It should also be interesting to try to ascertain why the fly or bait near the surface needs to be considerably smaller than the ones fished close to the bottom.

Remembering that economy of effort is of such vital importance to the salmon, and that a greater expenditure of energy is needed to take the fly near the surface than the one at eye-level, the factors which can show how that affects the position are perhaps the most relevant.

In very cold water, when the big springer is taken on the large bait or sunkfly, it is not unfair to say that even when it is reasonably certain that it is well rested, it puts up, relatively, a very poor fight compared with the small summer fish hooked near the surface. And, when the springer is beached, it will probably lie exhausted and motionless. The small fish later in the season, after an amazing exhibition of strength and determination, can still do plenty of twisting and kicking on the pebbles when it is brought ashore. It is apparent that in very cold water the salmon cannot generate nearly as much energy as it can at a higher temperature. The playing of a fish, of course, puts it to far greater sustained exertion than its natural requirements would ever be likely to call for; but how far it is capable of contending with that must be an indication of how much it will instinctively control the amount of energy used on any diversion from its prime purpose: for example, rising to a fly.

This seems to be confirmed by the disinclination of the fish to show voluntarily on the surface when the water is very cold, and its comparative willingness to do so at higher temperature; but another factor of considerable importance emerges at this juncture. In cold water the salmon usually lies in a steadier flow than when it is warmer. On starting to move, forward or upwards, it is undoubtedly able to use the force of the current beside it to help in gaining the necessary impetus, and therefore less effort is required to rise from a lie in a good flow than from one in slacker water. Consequently, not only has the salmon less energy to spare when the water is cold, but also it has less external assistance in rising to the surface.

There appears to be a satisfactory case, therefore, for assuming that those are the chief influences which decide the zone of interest of the salmon. The temperature of the water is the obvious key to the situation, and, as the readings of forty-two and forty-eight degrees Fahrenheit have emerged as a result of wide practical experience (though perhaps with slightly different perspectives of the target in mind), it must be accepted that they are of comprehensive significance. They can now be applied with full conviction.

As all sections of opinion imply agreement that forty-eight degrees is the minimum temperature, with the river at a reasonable level, at which greased-line fishing will offer the best prospects of sport with fly, we can accept that as an arbitrary figure marking approximately the end of the transitional period. After that the fly-fisher will have no thoughts of anything other than orthodox greased-lining.

There being no substantial evidence of worthwhile success with greased-line below forty-two degrees, but adequate proof of at least some sport at that temperature, we can be satisfied that there the transitional period applies. Probably it commenced at one or two degrees lower, say forty degrees, which would seem to be a very convenient reading, half-way between the coldest that water can be and the upper critical temperature of forty-eight degrees.

We now see three clearly defined phases of behaviour on the part of the salmon, each of which calls for a different approach by the angler. In the early days of the season, before the water reaches forty degrees, the fish are loth to rise at all; their attention is practically confined to their eye-level. From forty to forty-eight degrees the salmon may show some interest in lures at almost any level, but they take most freely in the general mid-water area. Above forty-eight degrees, they respond best to illusions in the vicinity of the surface of the water.

Spinning tackle is available which is suitable for all three periods. The methods of presenting the bait as satisfactorily as possible at all levels are commonly known, and there are no special difficulties attached to any of the phases which are not old and familiar enemies for most anglers. But in fly-fishing several difficulties still remain concerning the transitional period; but the discussion of those will be better done after consideration of the outstanding part of the original problem, that of reduction in the size of fly or bait as it becomes necessary to fish farther away from the bottom of the river.

Nobody will dispute that salmon take much larger flies and baits at eye-level than nearer the surface. Yet superficially

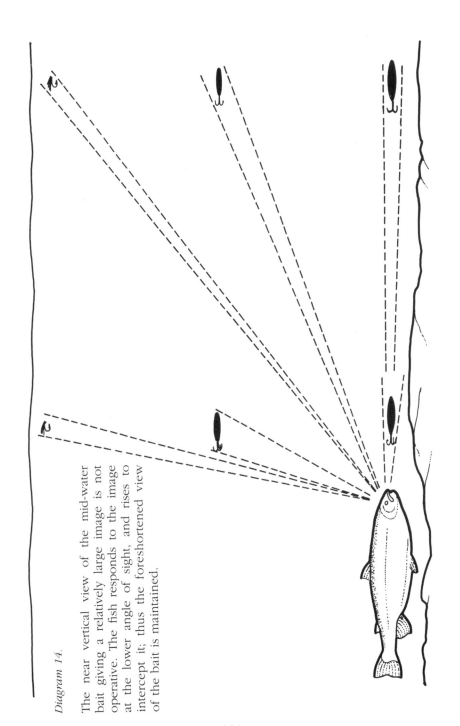

Diagram 14.

The near vertical view of the mid-water bait giving a relatively large image is not operative. The fish responds to the image at the lower angle of sight, and rises to intercept it; thus the foreshortened view of the bait is maintained.

this looks wrong. It would seem that the fish have a better opportunity to examine and be critical of the lure close to the bottom than the one that approaches near the surface and has to be observed through several feet of moving, perhaps turbulent, water.

There can be no doubt then that some other factors have a bigger influence on the image of the lure in the eye of the salmon than the mere matter of proximity. The angle of sight to the fly, as was discussed earlier in another context, suggests itself as being the agent that is responsible. As well as usually giving the salmon a foreshortened view of the fly or spinner, the low angle of sight results in the background being the darkest possible in the circumstances. On the other hand, the high angle of sight to the fly near the surface means that the more or less full size is seen, and that the background is the clearest in the salmon's horizon. It is not difficult to visualise that this diminishing or accentuating of the impact of the fly upon the sight of the fish is sufficient to account for the apparent contradiction of the sizes that are effective at the different levels. Thus we are able to reconcile the fact that, for example, in six feet of water and at their respective ranges, the three-inch lure at eye-level corresponds to the wooden devon of about two inches in mid-water and the one-inch fly just a little below the surface. (Diagram No. 14.)

So what the fly-fisher needs to do for a chance of sport during the transitionary period is easily understood; but there are several difficulties from the practical point of view.

Sunk-line equipment is not satisfactory for fishing the midwater area. A few fish can be caught, but it is too difficult to judge when the fly is fishing at the right level. Not much experience is needed to make it clear that something much more reliable is required.

Normal greased-line tackle has not proved to be much more successful. With the normal length of cast which can be used conveniently, it is necessary to have a relatively heavily weighted fly to ensure that it fishes satisfactorily at, say, three or four feet deep. Very soon that begins to drag the end of the line under, and, before long, too much of it is sinking for the depth at which the fly is fishing to be controlled properly.

Nevertheless, during the short spells when the fly has been fishing reasonably well, there has been sufficient response to justify efforts to evolve some modified method that will overcome the difficulties.

I now propose to whip a heavy, knotless, tapered cast to a self-floating line. Then, with the ordinary cast attached to the end, there should be a suitable length of nylon to enable a much less heavy fly to be fished deeply enough and at the same time remove the risk of a knot in the line fouling the end-ring. Any tendency of the whipping to cause the end of the line to be submerged should be a fairly constant factor. It would be unlikely to affect much of the line, and so would be no disadvantage.

If the main problem can be solved in that way, it should not take long to discover how heavy the flies will need to be to fish at the desired depths when the line is being controlled in much the same way as with orthodox greased-line fishing.

As the fly should fish considerably more slowly than the wooden devon, it can be anticipated that dressings of 1¼ to 1½ inches will be about right.

I feel rather optimistic about the prospects of this experiment, and it would be gratifying if it should prove to be the means of enabling an earlier effective start to the season on beats restricted to fly for those anglers who find sunk-line fishing to be too arduous.

Running Salmon

Several references have been made in earlier pages to the poor expectation of sport with salmon while they are actually running.

It cannot be denied that at least occasional fish are taken

when on the move in any river. There has been sufficient success of that sort in certain types of water to prove that it is not just a case of the odd, possibly defective, fish behaving contrary to an inflexible law. Nevertheless, in most places it is comparatively rare for moving fish to be caught.

The question arises, therefore, as to whether this can be reconciled with the oxygen theory. I think that if the full circumstances of running fish are considered, it cannot be thought that their behaviour is at all inconsistent with what is to be expected of them – even though they are at the maximum of alertness and, perhaps, not in an unresponsive mood.

We know that the salmon is well equipped to find the intricate route which it must follow to travel, as it must, in the most economical way. Consequently, there are no grounds for assuming that if it saw the angler's lure it would be too preoccupied for it to register. The kernel of the problem would seem to be, then, whether the moving fish is given enough opportunity to see the fly or bait in such a way as to make a big enough impact on it. And especially so when response to it would entail a time-wasting and laborious diversion from its path.

First, we will consider the position in medium-sized and small rivers which can only be fished from the banks when the water is high. No matter how slowly one tries to fish in those circumstances, the lure will not often remain in the proximity of the line of travel of the fish for long. Clearly, if sport is to be had, it is necessary that its presence there should coincide with the passing of the fish. That chance seems remote enough, but the position is frequently made much worse by the use of flies and baits which are much too small. Such a lure will probably look no different from the many little objects that are nearly always present in the water when the river is in spate. They will fail to create the necessary kind of illusion. On such a basis it is not surprising that so few fish are caught.

Now we will turn to the big, early rivers, where the fishing for the huge spring runs of salmon is done from boats. From long experience, either personal or handed down, the gillies know the drifts that will take them along the main lines of travel of the fish. And from a boat, the large fly or bait can be fished as slowly as desired – at the dangle if necessary. The wonderful catches which are so made are famous the world over.

In the case of an individual salmon taken, it could not be said with certainty that it was a runner, a resting fish, or a resident. But often when sport is particularly hectic, the fish can be seen to be travelling, and there seems to be no doubt at all that this system of fishing kills a lot of salmon while they are actually moving up the river.

The method that should be adopted for bank fishing is now pretty obvious. Casts should be selected where the set of the current will facilitate extremely slow fishing in an area through which the fish will pass. The lure should be big enough to command attention. There is nothing to be gained by the angler gradually moving downstream when the fish are travelling up to meet him, so when a favourable place has been found there is no point in leaving it.

Such tactics will not appeal much to many anglers; but the occasions when they are needed do not occur very frequently, and they would be sufficiently interesting to make a trial to secure first-hand proof that running fish are not non-takers.

The reader will appreciate that although this section looks, perhaps, out of place here, it involves factors discussed at various previous stages, and could not therefore have been dealt with as briefly before now.

Spinning

Sometimes I am accused of bias in favour of fly-fishing. I admit that I find the magic of fishing-tackle is most enthralling when it is for fly-fishing, and I cannot imagine anything to compare with the delight of greased-line fishing in favourable circumstances. But the problem of salmon fishing is exactly the same whether the artificial lure is fly or bait – the combination of size and colour, the distance from the bottom at which it is fished, its behaviour in relation to the current, must result in the creation of a suitable illusion. But of what we do not know.

Most of us on occasions find that the weight of lure that will give best prospects, in the prevailing circumstances, can be cast and controlled most easily with spinning gear. Then there is no reason why we should have to look for any other explanation for the use of that method.

Similarly there are times when the weight of the lure that will fish best at the speed and depth required can be thrown and regulated most conveniently with fly-fishing tackle. And then that alone is the justification for employing that style of fishing.

Any inferiority or superiority in the illusion to which the salmon responds cannot relate to whether the human eye sees it as a fly or a spinner, and there cannot therefore be any difference on aesthetic grounds. We ought to be able to indulge our personal biases without false complications, and it should not deprive them of their pleasurableness to recognise that such is all that they are.

I have not gone into much detail about spinning tactics, because my frank view is that if spinning cannot be done correctly with facility, the nature of the lures and lines used are such that it is not possible to do it correctly at all on a fully controlled and consistent basis. In other words, there are fairly strict limitations to what can be done with any particular type of bait. It requires some experience to get the normal performance out of it; no amount of skill can make it do more.

When I spin I try to cover the lies in exactly the same way as I should wish to do with a fly, and when spinning equipment will not permit that, I use the tackle that will. Although the change to fly gives me no regret, neither does it arise from any higher motives as far as my intentions towards the fish are concerned.

A most important aspect of the relationship between spinning and fly-fishing that is not always fully appreciated is that the results achieved with the one method are most informative data for application to the other. An attempt to analyse the sort of illusion which proves successful can always be helpful in trying to achieve the same thing in the other way.

One aspect of spinning which gives scope for valuable study is that of spoon-baits and adaptations of their principle. They provide proof – apparently more so than with any other lure – that the salmon responds to what it thinks it sees, and not to the actual article that is being offered to it.

This pronounced capacity of the spoon to create an illusion has been exploited extensively in all directions – size, shape, weight, reflection, colour and sonic qualities. There is little that the angler could wish of a spoon which is not available. But although the best kinds of such baits for some special circumstances are quite commonly known, there remains a strong tendency, when an alternative seems necessary, to try this and that without any particular progressive policy in mind.

Again I will say that with fly and spinner the problem is basically the same. The colour categories of spoon-baits (and of course of other spinners), should be regarded in much the same way as was suggested for flies. The popular preferences of anglers for certain categories of spoons for particular conditions of the river – such as brown and gold, or black and gold, for a coloured water – are based on the greater success they have had in the circumstances than other combinations have had. Most of these established favourites will, I think, be found to be confirmation of the advantages to be gained by using the method of selection which has been discussed.

I am inclined to feel that with most spoons too much emphasis is put on the need for brilliant reflection. Perhaps on occasions the silvers and golds cannot be overdone, but I think that the less shiny ones should always be tried first.

As for shape, I think there are many occasions when more attention to slenderness would be an advantage, and the angler should aim at more versatility in this respect than is provided by the contents of the majority of tackle-cases.

The effectiveness of sonic qualities in lures in some circumstances cannot be denied, but whether this is of any general benefit in salmon-fishing is questionable. If a fish were taking a lure under the influence of the instinct to destroy a small injured creature it would seem that the emitting of a vibration by the bait could be of value. But the question arises as to how much stress is necessary in this respect, whether all spinning baits have not automatically got this quality – and perhaps to as great a degree as is required.

Certainly when salmon are in a responsive mood and can be taken on any suitable fly or spinner, the intentional incorporation of sonic qualities into the lure is obviously quite unnecessary. Therefore, we can safely reserve our judgment on this question until more information is available on the measurement of the sonic value of lures.

Finally, fly-fishers and spinners can be equally guilty – perhaps unthinkingly, of course – of constantly over-fishing the lies. The policy which offers the best prospects of sport will always leave the pool well worth fishing by the rod that follows shortly afterwards. If the novice will discipline himself in that respect, it will be of great value to him throughout his fishing career, and not only so in the sport he will enjoy with the salmon.

My current problem

No angler should need to offer any assurances of his sincerity in his efforts to get a better understanding of fishing, and on that score, I have no misgiving about this report.

What I do regret, though, is that due to my shortcomings, it is devoid of the colour that is the right of any discussion on fishing.

It is, indeed, fortunate for me that the reader will be an angler for whom even plain words about salmon fishing will perhaps create in his imagination a background of the charms of the rivers with which he is familiar and the fascination of the wonderful story of that splendid fish.

If, in that way, these pages are helped to be readable, I shall be very thankful.

Glossary of Terms and Notes

Cold-blooded

This term means that the body produces no heat of its own and is dependent on its environment for any warmth. Therefore it has no specific temperature requirement to ensure its correct functioning.

By conduction a fish assumes the varying temperature of the water surrounding it, and presumably is indifferent as far as actual heat is concerned to the gradual changes that occur.

The fact that a fish does not have to burn up reserves of energy to produce bodily warmth is the reason why it can go for long periods without food and suffer no ill effects. In the case of a salmon, this is no doubt an essential factor in its ability to withstand the extremely long fast in freshwater.

Drag

In greased-line fishing the fly is said to be dragging when it ceases to fish correctly because of some unwanted resistance or side-pull of the line. In other words, the behaviour of the fly is no longer under the control of the angler.

In recent years there have been many arguments to the effect that it is wrong to talk about avoiding drag, because it is actually a certain degree of drag that causes the fly to fish correctly and that without it the fly would drift lifelessly.

Whatever may be said of the correctness of such state-
ments, they nevertheless serve no useful purpose. Anglers
do not talk about giving the fly a little more drag; they refer
to more check or more lead, and those two words are more
explicit as to the intention as well.

I suggest, therefore, that the use of the word drag should
he restricted, as it used to be, to the occasions when control
of the fly has been lost.

Backing-up and Stripping

Although most commonly known for their employment in
deep, slack, or very steady water, these methods can be
applied advantageously elsewhere.

The fly is usually cast rather squarely across the pool. In
stripping, the line is recovered by the left hand in draws
of about a yard at a time, or by coiling the line in the
hand, preferably in a figure of eight. When backing-up, a
somewhat similar result is achieved by holding the rod fairly
high and steady, and, while continuing to face the area of
water being fished, the angler steps backwards at an even
pace along the edge of the river in an upstream direction.

It is quite remarkable that though this must often result in
the salmon seeing a great deal of the line as it passes over
or close to him before the fly is eventually within his reach,
he takes it.

Although the fish will certainly see the line when it drops
on the water, however, it will then look to be stationary
or just drifting, and he will not realise that it is actually
moving along its own axis. Perhaps the sudden appearance
of the line absorbs his attention to the extent of his failing
at that time also to notice the arrival of the fly. When,
shortly afterwards, the fly reaches a point where it arouses
the salmon's interest, it seems that any shock experienced
by him, due to the disturbance of the line falling on to the
water, must have been dispelled, and then the continued

presence of the apparently inert line must no longer cause any distraction.

The difference in the behaviour of the fly during backing-up and stripping is only slight, and does not amount to much more than a greater change in direction as it moves through the water when backing-up. Nevertheless there are occasions when that appears to have much more attraction for the fish than the action produced by stripping.

To the spectator, both methods appear to be very simple, but many anglers – myself included – find it impossible to get into the way of backing-up comfortably and successfully, even in the least difficult circumstances. The few adepts seem to be unhampered by treacherous going underfoot and they are able to concentrate absolutely on their purpose. No doubt they see many more situations calling for backing-up than would the angler less nimble in the execution of this method.

Some of the outstanding exponents of backing-up can even make their flies cover lies in fast current exactly as they wish – that is a delightful thing to watch. The way in which the fly then moves ahead of the salmon from behind it sometimes proves to be irresistible and will produce sport when little else will work.

Any angler who finds that he has the natural aptitude for backing-up enjoyably should certainly foster it and exploit his good fortune to the full.

At first, stripping requires a little practice to get used to the manipulation of the line with the left hand, but it is easily mastered by any angler and can be extremely useful in all sorts of situations. Variations and modified ways of stripping are often invaluable aids in conjunction with ordinary greased-line techniques. For example, on many occasions when it is normal to resort to mending downstream, the desired objective can be achieved much more effectively by the combined use of the current and gentle stripping.

Mending

This is the procedure by which the greased-line is repositioned on the water so that the fly will traverse correctly the lie being fished, and will not be led round too quickly or checked too much.

The line above the cast is lifted clear of the water and swung over two or three yards, all of which is done in one progressive movement. When it is executed skilfully, the fly remains undisturbed and continues to fish as required throughout.

In addition to the disadvantage of the disturbance, however, mending has a marked tendency to make the line sink, and therefore it should not be used indiscriminately.

For some reason or other, mending seems to have become something of a ritual with some greased-line fishers. Because of that, the novice should realise that although skill in this manoeuvre is a valuable asset, it is the least desirable of the various possible means by which the fly can usually be made to behave as is required.

I venture to say that had nobody ever thought of the idea of mending in the currently accepted way, greased-line fishers in general would have developed their resources with other techniques to the extent of their being able to. do all that is necessary more efficiently and effectively.

Grilse

This is the name given to a salmon which has certain peculiarities of behaviour and physical characteristics.

After the normal kind of salmon has migrated to the sea as a smolt, it does not return to the river until a minimum of two years has elapsed, but the grilse makes its reappearance after a little over one year.

A grilse can easily be identified by its forked tail as against the square-ended one of the salmon. Also the wrist of the grilse's tail is much more slender and the muscles are not nearly so well developed. When a salmon is tailed (lifted by the tail with the hand, keeping the thumb and forefinger uppermost) the hold is very secure, but the tail of the grilse tends to slip through one's grip.

Runs of grilse usually commence in the late spring or early summer, and are most common in rivers which also have good runs of seatrout. Grilse are usually around five or six pounds, but they cannot be identified by weight alone, because small summer salmon often weigh as little or less than some of the grilse.

Often one hears grilse called young or immature salmon, but they are certainly not immature, because they spawn in the normal way.

Whether or not a grilse is correctly described as a young salmon is another matter. At least one salmon expert says, "Once a grilse, always a grilse!" That implies that grilse retain their characteristic tail construction throughout their lives and that it can be recognised during any subsequent trip to the river to spawn. Others of the scientists claim that a grilse is only correctly so-called when it makes its first return to the river and that subsequently it is a normal salmon in all respects.

It seems strange that these days there should still be any doubt about a point like this. I hope that soon we shall be told much more about this very interesting question by the authorities on the subject.

Salmon – clean, stale, red and potted

A salmon is generally classed as a clean fish so long as it retains a fairly silvery coat. Some anglers use the term only in reference to absolutely fresh-run fish, but that is too great a restriction.

Stale describes a salmon when obviously it can no longer be regarded as fresh-run. The word is often used rather loosely, though, to include all such fish, clean and otherwise, thus I think, robbing the word of its value and I prefer the interpretation that a stale fish, although not fresh-run, is still clean.

A coloured, or red fish, is one that has started to acquire its spawning coat.

Potted means that the fish has been in the same pool for rather a long time. Ideas of what constitutes a long time, however, vary considerably. On the lower reaches, where fresh-run fish are plentiful, three or four days as residents in a pool are sometimes enough for the salmon to be regarded as potted, but on the higher reaches that somewhat disparaging term would not usually be used until a very much longer time had elapsed.

Skull-dragging

In its crudest form, this means hauling a fish out on strong tackle with its head furrowing through the water.

There is one unusual method of landing a salmon which could almost be called extremely refined skull-dragging. Some anglers are quite adept at it, particularly on the spate streams, but most rods would only think of trying it for the sake of satisfying a desire to have achieved it at least once.

Apart from the practical value of this trick – which it really is – it is extremely interesting as the means of proving that the salmon has no work to do when it is at rest in its lie and very little indeed when it is moving. In order to make this clearer, it will be better first to describe "walking a fish up", which is a common practice, but has not been mentioned in this text.

Often it is found that after a period of fighting strongly, a fish comes under steady control, but the position is not suitable for landing it, while a little higher up there is a favourable spot. If a steady pressure is applied in as nearly an upstream direction as possible, and the angler moves off slowly, keeping the line tight, and walks in the upstream direction, the fish follows with no added pressure being felt on the tackle. It is really so easy that some anglers quite unconcernedly put their rods over their shoulders and march off for forty or fifty yards without any trouble. Perhaps when the fish is then turned side-on to the current with a view to beaching it, it will put up a little more resistance, but it is seldom of any avail to it following the walking-up process.

Now to describe the method of landing a fish referred to earlier. When a salmon is hooked after returning to its lie with the fly, it usually remains perfectly still for several seconds before moving off to counter the application of side strain. If, however, the angler is fishing from a suitable place for beaching, and quickly increasing strain is applied in an upstream direction, the fish begins to follow just as in walking-up. Then before the salmon has had time to collect its wits, so to speak, it is raced up and swerved round on to the dry pebbles. It is given no chance to get any purchase on the water to resist sufficiently, and therefore cannot prevent this rapid conclusion to the encounter.

Speed, full use of the length of the rod, and a bit of quick footwork are necessary, and, needless to say, the angler must be ready to change his plan instantly and let the fish run if he sees that he is not going to succeed in turning the fish towards the beach without overstraining the tackle. An opportunist adaptation of this can often be used to advantage while playing a fish, with beaching in view, if the salmon comes towards the rod quickly. The reel cannot usually be used fast enough to exploit the chance when it arises, and a hurried retreat across the pebbles is required. But the salmon will often finish up high and dry, yards away from the water's edge.

Such events are clear evidence that the salmon has no work to do to maintain its position in the current when lying in the place of its choice. If that were not the case, all it would have to do at the commencement of being brought upstream after being hooked would be to cease the effort. And that would add an equivalent amount of strain to that already necessary for the rod to apply to move it forward. Then the angler would feel the extra resistance, which would probably make it impossible to get the fish moving sufficiently well.

It has occurred to me when thinking of the way in which a salmon seems to stay in the same line of current when being walked-up, that it is like a knife going along the grain through a piece of wood. The grain in the current would have been a very useful expression to use when discussing how a salmon runs.

Commentaries

By Terry Thomas

For many years I fished principally for trout. I fished for salmon when conditions were right, or when I was invited to fish specifically for them. Because I was almost born with a rod in my hand and had been taught to cast as soon as I was big enough, I could put my fly or bait more or less where I wanted it. Inevitably I caught fish, particularly when salmon were "on". On those too rare occasions they will take your hat if you throw it at them nicely.

The worst possible training for a salmon fisherman is to fish for trout. The trout fisherman thinks only of the top of the water: the salmon angler must understand the water from the surface to the river bed. The best upbringing for salmon fishing is years of float fishing, preferably on very different types of river. A good float fisherman must understand what goes on beneath the surface and must be able to "read" the speed of sub-surface currents as well as control his line on the top. His problems are in many cases identical with those of the salmon fisher.

I learned more about salmon fishing when with some friends I rented a short stretch of the Usk for seven or eight years. Here, at least, I had the advantage of continuity. It was a high-water beat, and after a year or two we learned from pooled experience what type of fly or devon to fish at different water heights. Salmon fishing on this water became

128

a lot less of a gamble: elsewhere it was still for me largely a matter of chance.

It was during my tenure of this Usk fishing that I first met Reg Righyni. He is one of those fortunate people who excel at most things. As a young man he had been an outstanding match fisherman. Progressing to trout fishing, the most logical of all forms of fishing, he soon became equally good with wet or dry fly. Taking up salmon fishing he was not content to accept that success or failure lay always in the lap of the gods. He insisted there must be a logical reason why salmon will suddenly all come on the take and equally some reason why at times they are quite uncatchable.

To begin with I had not the slightest faith in his ideas. They seemed to me no more likely than all the other theories put forward to account for the apparently inconsistent behaviour of *Salmo salar*. But the more I talked with Righyni, and argued with him, usually until the early hours, and the more we fished together, the more and more convinced I became that here was the answer.

I cannot remember now whether it was Bernard Venables or I or both who suggested that a book should be written on this subject, or whether Reg decided himself. Eventually, however, it was completed. Bernard and I told him it was not enough. The ideas in it should be supported by actual experiences. I even went so far as to offer to collaborate in a general book on salmon fishing based on the taking times theory.

On this point Reg Righyni was quite adamant. He had written all he was going to write. I argued about this with him many times and one night, when the whisky was low in the decanter, I tried the line about his responsibilities to the sport. He had a duty, I said, to pass on these ideas in the strongest form, a duty to other fishermen as a means of expressing his gratitude for the pleasures he had had from fishing. I had reckoned without the cunning of the man. So it was a matter of sacred duty, was it? Well, he was not going to do any more and if I felt so very strongly about it, I had better do it myself. I should have done what any uncatchable fish does: I should have kept my mouth shut.

Every now and again, then, when I have some experience which bears out some idea in this book, I have made a short commentary. I hope these commentaries will support and make clearer the ideas which are Reg Righyni's and Reg Righyni's alone.

Commentary A

As a small boy I was on holiday with my family on the Usk. One bright August morning, William Law, the keeper of the Buckland water, arrived, bidding my father bring his salmon rod with him, as there was a good chance of a fish. I started trout fishing, and although the only sport we had been having had been in the evening, I started catching trout. Then, hearing a whistling and the sound of Law's dog barking, I ran down to a pool below in time to see my father grassing a salmon. The trout were rising well, too, and I remember being so excited I could not hold a fly still enough to knot it on to my cast. Suddenly it all stopped, and Law suggested we might well go home until the evening. We didn't, of course, but Law was right. The river settled back into its normal August torpor. The next day I asked whether we would catch a salmon again. No, said Law, it was not worthwhile trying; nor was it on any other day during the rest of the week.

Years later I reminded him of this occasion and asked him why on one day preceded and followed by apparently identical days he knew that a salmon was catchable. He told me he could give no reason – he just knew conditions were suddenly right.

Years later still, I was talking to the late Herbert Hatton of Hereford, who knew more about catching salmon than most people. He told me that when, suddenly, you hear all the birds burst into song, that is the time a fish will take.

It was not until I met Reg Righyni a few years ago and I listened to his ideas that these two incidents and many other similar ones began to fit into pattern. We all experience days when we feel on top of the world, and animals run round bursting with energy. Surely it is logical that fish feel the same. Fish of course are particularly sensitive to the amount of oxygen. Either too much or too little and they become light-headed or lethargic. Why do trout suddenly start to move into position before a hatch of fly? Sometimes they will move up fifty yards or more to be in a position where they can most easily intercept their prey, or where they know nymphs are going to "hatch". The only reason for this must be that they know that the amount of oxygen is right to provide conditions for an eclosion.

Why, too, in spring do we notice "burst hatches" of fly? Suddenly for a few minutes down come the march browns or the spring olives in droves. Equally suddenly the hatch stops. Half an hour later there is another burst just for a few minutes, then again it stops. These bursts must surely be the result of just the right amount of oxygen for short periods. It is a fact that these hatches generally coincide with salmon taking times.

Since starting these commentaries I have had a considerable amount of correspondence with fishermen who cannot understand how a salmon can survive a year or more without feeding. In very much a layman's way I tried to point out how a cold-blooded animal like a salmon with a year or more of sea feeding behind it, seeking always a position in the stream where it uses the minimum of energy will not need to "take on more fuel" to replace that energy. My ten-year-old daughter was the cause of my seeing other examples of somewhat similar animal behaviour.

She had just returned from the home of a zoologist friend where a small boa-constrictor was kept. What did they feed it on, I enquired? On mice, was the answer but it needed little food. It would eat a mouse, then go to sleep for some weeks until the mouse was digested and the snake felt hungry again and woke up. Here was a very close parallel to a salmon's behaviour and a look at one or two books of reference on reptiles showed this pattern to be common. In one of the works, however, my attention was drawn to the again similar behaviour of warm-blooded animals which hibernate.

These animals, having acquired enough fat by heavy summer feeding to last them the winter, find themselves a cave or a hole or some similar holt and curl up and go to sleep. At this point their body temperature drops until they are nearly cold-blooded and their heart-beat decelerates as does their breathing. Their whole metabolism slows down so that they use a minimum of energy.

Here surely is a very close parallel to a salmon, which alas!! for long periods sometimes seems to be in a state of trance. Give your hibernating bear a change in the weather, a warmer spell in midwinter and he will wake up and maybe hunt round for some more food. Given a mild day in December the bats will come out to hawk whatever insects they can find. What we have to discover is what wakes the salmon from his state of trance. To me now there can only be one possible answer.

Commentary B

There are two points here on wind.

Firstly I do not agree that wind makes it difficult to create a suitable illusion. Fish will take very tiny flies in the roughest water of a run, and if the correct illusion is created in such turbulent water, I cannot see how wind will prevent the same thing happening. On lochs and still pools, wind is, of course, essential for sport.

Secondly, while many Scottish streams are loch fed to some lesser or greater amount, the same is not true of many other rivers, so the effect of wind on lochs may not be clear to many fishermen. A strong breeze from the right direction pushes water out of the loch and causes the river to rise.

Author's reply to Commentary B

Let me refer to the first point mentioned by Terry Thomas about wind and the creation of a suitable illusion. I am glad that this has been brought up, because a lot of people will – at first – undoubtedly agree with Terry Thomas. I am sure, nevertheless, that there is much truth in my view, and that Terry is under-estimating some of the essential factors which, if considered more fully, may induce some revision of his opinion.

First, however, I wish to stress that I did say "strong wind", and I agree that a good breeze is generally helpful in the creation of a suitable illusion. Also, in a strong current, where the wind does not alter the contour of the surface of the water much, nor the way the fly fishes providing that the angler is still able to control his line satisfactorily, the wind does not matter very much.

It is in the deeper water where the speed of the current is not strong enough to prevent big, rolling waves that sport is spoilt, and where a lull in the wind often results in a fish being caught. The comparison of such pools with still water is not as pertinent as it seems to be, because strong wind has a very different influence on still water from that on moving water.

To clarify the position, it is necessary to consider separately the influence of the wind on the three classes of water previously mentioned, but in seemingly the wrong sequence.

First we will take the fast current. We endeavour to make the fly simulate a small, perhaps injured, creature, which is battling with the current and gradually losing ground if the current is too strong, but always heading into the current.

Providing the wind allows us to do this, a suitable illusion is created and fish will be caught if a taking time is in progress. If the strength or direction of the wind prevents adequate control of the fly, the chances of sport suffer accordingly.

In still water strong wind causes a current on and near the surface. If observation is kept on an article submerged a few inches, it will be seen that it is drifting at the speed of a current in approximately the same direction as the wind. A small swimming creature would head into this current most of the time and could perhaps gain ground, even at a tangent to the flow. If the fly can be made to do that, as would be easy when boat fishing, the illusion created would be suitable.

Now we come to a deepish, gently flowing pool, and we find an entirely different situation. A light article, such as a dry leaf, which is floating high on the water, will go in the direction of the wind, but a sunk leaf, an inch or so down, will be seen to be moving in the direction of the current as if there were no wind on the water. This shows clearly that although the wind can agitate the surface violently, it has practically no influence on the flow of the water. Consequently, the small creature that the fly is supposed to simulate would behave exactly the same as if there were no wind. On such pools, it is difficult enough to control the line to make the fly swim properly without the interference of strong wind, but where that is present, it is usually beyond the powers of the most skilful angler to compensate for it and keep his fly behaving satisfactorily for any length of time.

Clearly, it is largely a matter of line control. In a fast current, the difficulties are often not too great, and in still water fishing it is easy for a good angler, but in the gentle current of a steady pool it is even more difficult than it seems to be, which is evidenced by the fact that fish are so often taken in sheltered places or during lulls in the wind, and very rarely when the surface of a gently flowing pool is very rough.

Apart from the question of line control, though, I believe that salmon do not like billowing waves, and even when practising backing-up in slack or dead water, it is a good ripple that is wanted and not rollers. In my opinion, the scale of the variation in the background is so great when there are big long waves, that a small object like a fly does not create sufficient impression on the fish to attract the kind of attention that sets reflex action in motion. The more settled background during the lulls enables the fly to have a more striking image, and one that can create a suitable illusion.

Commentary C

A word on spates. Not all rivers become highly acid in spate. The chalk streams are perhaps the best examples of exceptions. It is rare to see one of these streams coloured. It is all a matter of the type of terrain they drain, of course.

The Usk and the Wye, in their middle and lower reaches at any rate, never run with a peaty, port-wine stain. They run brown or red. In consequence fish can be caught in a really dirty spate.

Local knowledge and observation are the two vital factors for catching salmon in dirty water. You want to know where their running path is, and even more important, where a fish is liable to stop and rest.

On the water I used to fish on the Usk, we had one perfect spate catch. The cast was across the tail of a long pool, just before a series of rapids. Running fish would often halt for a while here, sometimes well under one's own bank. On a number of occasions we have had four fish in a day from this one stand, when most fellow fishermen had not even bothered to put up a rod.

Spate fishing is a boring business. It is a question of sticking to one place and fishing into water where you can see little. Fish, too, are often tired and give little fight. The ideal to aim at is a cast where your bait – and a spoon is the best spate lure – will cover possible resting fish and cross the running path.

There are worse things, too, than peaty spates. On the Usk, for example, there is a little tributary, the Clydach, which drains an area containing quarries. When it comes down in spate it runs grey and turns the main river the same colour. Clydach water completely deadens the river. Even the proverbial "blind 'uns" or "daft 'uns" are then uncatchable.

Commentary D

The points in this section bring out the importance of keeping records. A salmon-fishing diary makes both interesting reading later and, more important, does provide a means of compiling data, particularly about one stretch of water.

Normally the advice has been to record heights of water, water temperature, where, at what time and on what lure the fish was taken, its weight of course, and other less vital facts such as how long you took to kill it.

I can think of no field in which history repeats itself more often than in salmon fishing. Just think for example how many fish are hooked in exactly the same place. If you know a stretch of water really well, you can predict what will happen on a short-term basis.

I cannot recall having read anywhere the sort of evidence which Reg Righyni has just described. If you include in your diary the weather factors, you are compiling the sort of information which does enable the observant fisherman to predict when and where he is going to catch a fish.

One final point. Reg's remarks about lines floating and not floating were written before the floating line became an efficient piece of tackle. With such lines the behaviour mentioned does not of course occur.

Commentary E

I think the preceding section is probably the most valuable part of this book.

Before I started to fish with Reg Righyni I never had bothered to consider what caused a river to flow. Since I had been taught how an internal-combustion engine works, I had the necessary knowledge of gravity and suction. As basically a top-of-the-water fly fisherman for trout I had just not bothered to work things out.

I had, of course, learned to understand current. The problems of drag, the feeding lies of trout, as apart from their non-feeding lies, the suction which pulls down a floating line, all these were learned from experience and all were part of the concern with what happened at the top. Although I worked out an effective method of sunk line fishing for trout, I had never considered that the water at the bottom was behaving very differently from the water at the surface.

In this ignorance of water behaviour I was certainly not alone, even among those who wrote books on trout fishing. In so many of these you will find sketches of where trout lie. Most of these sketches will have small boulders sticking out of the water with trout tucked in behind them. Experience soon taught me that I rarely caught trout in such pockets and I did take the trouble to note that turbulence would make it extremely uncomfortable for any fish to lie in many of these "points of vantage". Equally I found that where the current was such that a trout would lie behind a rock, the fish would often be facing in a general downstream direction. The boulder had swung the current sometimes until it was flowing in the opposite direction to the main current. The trout was therefore facing the right way to enable it to hold itself in the current, to breathe easily and to intercept its food. In the books you will find every fish facing up river!

I was not therefore alone in my ignorance, and when the obvious was suddenly explained to me, I wondered whether my lack of observation was general. So I carried out a little test.

I asked some questions of four experienced trout and salmon fishermen. It soon became obvious that, like me, they had never bothered to consider the behaviour of water although, once they started to think about it, they all had the necessary knowledge to work out how and why a river flowed and how and why the currents varied in speed between top and bottom.

I then asked the same sort of questions of four float fishermen. They were all men with much less education and, generally, I would think, lesser powers of observation. Their whole art, however, was based on this differing water behaviour and they had a very clear three-dimensional picture of the river as against the two-dimensional picture of the surface fishermen. For years they had been shotting their casts so that they could, for instance, pierce the fast top water and present their bait in a natural fashion to the fish in the slower water at the bottom.

I think then it is reasonable to assume that there must be many anglers who are just as unobservant as I was. The preceding remarks on river flow must have provided the basis for assessing the behaviour of different types of water. Let us then look at practical ways of learning to read a river.

A little experimenting on any salmon pool with hookless float tackle will reveal the different current speeds at different depths. Better still, winter bait fishing for grayling will teach the same practical lessons in river reading with the added interest of catching fish which behave like salmon. Float fishing for grayling is the closest form of fishing to fly fishing for salmon. Control of the line is essential to avoid drag, and thus, the unnatural behaviour of the bait. It is, of course, much more difficult to "mend" a two-pound line than a fly line. Furthermore, grayling, like salmon, lie on or near the bottom and must rise to take bait or fly. Righyni, needless to say, is a master at this type of fishing. Any form of float fishing gives this sort of instruction in current understanding; but grayling fishing is best of all, for grayling rivers are usually identical in nature with salmon rivers.

There is an old army axiom that time spent on reconnaissance is seldom wasted. It applies equally to fishing, and, above all, salmon fishing. Reconnaissance is of two kinds – strategical and tactical.

If you are fortunate enough to be the owner or lessee of a salmon fishing, or to fish the same beat frequently, then you can and should reconnoitre the whole of the fishing on a strategical basis. The time to do this is when the water is dead low, and the bare bones of the river's skeleton revealed. Time spent in waders and with polaroid glasses will mean more fish killed when conditions are right, and, more important, much more interest, for you will be fishing with a feel for the river and not, as so often happens, fishing blind.

When you are fishing on holiday or have just the odd day on a stretch of salmon water, your whole desire will be to get in as much fishing as time permits. You will still do better to study each pool before you fish it.

A season or two ago I was fishing with Reg Righyni on the Newton Hall stretch of the Lune. This is difficult water to know well because here the river flows through a broad valley and the pools alter every year and indeed during the year. I had just taken a fish from the Middle Pool and we had moved on to the Bottom Pool, some two hundred yards downstream. From this lower vantage point, Reg pointed out to me that by looking upstream I could see the shape of the Middle Pool as though I was looking at a contour map of it. The water diverted by every under-water obstruction to the flow showed up as though etched in ink, and most of the likely holding water therefore was clearly identifiable by these dark patches.

Time spent on tactical reconnaissance, looking up at the pool from below from water level, is never wasted, even on a short and long-anticipated fishing day.

Commentary F

The points about reconnaissance made in the previous commentary apply equally to understanding river flow and to locating lies. Wading a pool at low water and studying the bottom with the help of polaroids enables you to know both exactly where salmon lie and why they lie there.

If you know the pool reasonably well, you will know the places where salmon are hooked. If you are able to wade out to them you will see why they hold fish. Often, as Reg Righyni points out, the holding area will be void of vegetation, due to fish having rested there.

Whenever possible, salmon prefer to have a rock bottom under them. Next in preference, all things being equal, is a bottom of large stones, and then smaller gravel. Fish do not like sand, silt or mud, although I know one place on the Usk where, in high summer and at low water, salmon can be seen in some numbers in a slack bay with a heavy bottom covering of silt. A spring of very cold water enters the river here and this, I imagine, is the attraction.

When there has been a heavy run of salmon and a large number of fish are in the river, they will be found inhabiting all sorts of "new" lies. There will be a great deal of jostling for the more usual resting places; fish are hard to interest, and productive casts often very unproductive. It very definitely pays under these circumstances to try the other possible holding areas. Reconnaissance with polaroids will often show fish in places where they have rarely or never been seen before.

Let me tell of two or three practical examples of low water

study of salmon pools. There was one pool I used to fish where there was, for the first two or three seasons of our tenure, an almost certain taking place when the river was right. It was a very easy place to mark for there was a bush on our bank and an outcrop of rock on the other one. It was the sort of place where you astonish non-fishing friends by pointing out beforehand where you were going to catch them a fish.

Then this cast stopped producing and for several years we did not take a fish there. One winter we had some tremendous floods and the next year the old lie started to hold fish again. As soon as we had some low water I waded out and examined the bottom. There I found two saucer-like depressions in rock. In the non-productive years these must have been covered up by gravel and in this state offered no advantage to the fish.

On the same pool, particularly when the "saucers" were non-productive, we noticed that if a fish showed at the tail you would almost certainly catch one straight away at the head. If you did not have an offer there, you shot off to the tail and almost certainly caught a fish there. Examination at low water showed that the most attractive-looking holt was at the head where a large rock produced the sort of ideal lie which Reg has described. There was also a lie at the tail, although there was no obvious reason for it. Whether the fish showed at the tail when entering the pool or before settling down at the tail I do not know. I am, however, sure that it first went up to the best lie at the top, and if it was tenanted dropped back to the Number Two position. I remember so well working this trick with Bernard Venables. We were putting up our rods at the top of the pool when a fish showed at the tail. I told him to stop what he was doing, to get in at the head and if he didn't have a fish straight away, to hare off and cast where we had seen the fish. First covering cast he had a nineteen-pounder. Those are the sort of fish you feel you have caught and not the ones which catch you.

There was one other lie which always mystified me, particularly as fish suddenly stopped using it or rather them. There was a shallow stretch of river; gravel on our side, gravel and rock on the other. In summer you could wade across in gum boots. The first few seasons, before the fish for no apparent reason gave up using the lies, we often saw and sometimes caught fish there. Examination showed two depressions in the rock, each about the size of a household bath. I still cannot fathom why salmon should choose to rest there when there were many other much more secure-looking holts available. Incidentally it was not a case of the river being full of fish, with unusual lies tenanted.

Commentary G

On dull days, when fish are really on the take, the choice of fly is less important and fish are caught, generally all about the same time, on flies varying greatly in size. These are the days when fish will "take your hat" if you throw it at them nicely. Most experienced salmon fishermen will remember odd days like this. The best example I can recall was on the Don. As a fisherman on the other bank landed a fish on a 1/0 Jock Scott so a friend on ours hooked one on a size 12 Silver March Brown with which he was fishing for trout. On bright days it can be very different.

I well remember taking a friend for a day to the Wye at Ballingham. His sole fishing experience was catching roach as a boy but he is one of those fortunate people who pick up things quickly and half an hour on the golf course had him putting out a more than adequate line.

We started out on the glide at Rock Cottage. It was a hot, very bright day and as I had had a fish a few days previously under apparently identical conditions, on a size 8 Haslam, I tied on the same fly again. You fish this glide off a shingle beach with a high bank behind and, as this presented casting difficulties to my companion, we arranged that I should fish down to the beginning of the run, where there is no obstacle to the back cast, and that he should take over there.

To cut a long story short, we moved nine fish in a row, some of them several times. Fish after fish rose to the fly and not one took hold. I did what I thought was right and put on a finer cast and moved down my fly sizes until I had the smallest fly in my box on the end.

Then, in desperation, I walked upstream and looked at the gauge. In those days I related size of fly or bait to water height and as the river was higher than I had thought, I put on a size 4 Invicta. Almost first cast I had a fish and immediately afterwards my friend had another to give him the fortunate record of a fish first time out.

What I had done, all unwittingly, was to mount a Silhouette fly that the fish could still see despite the dazzle. They were of course losing sight of the small slender flies as they rose to take them. This experience bears out Reg's advice that if a fish misses a fly, move up in size, not down.

As Reg Righyni rightly says, salmon flies are still in a state of evolution. At this juncture then, it might be wise to look at their history.

The story of the salmon fly is, of necessity, one of trial and error. This must surely be the only way to invent lures for a fish which feeds neither actively nor regularly in fresh water.

The man who has had most influence on the salmon fly must be Kelson, if for no other reason than that his dressings have been so faithfully followed by professional fly makers. Kelson, in the 'eighties, advocated bright gaudy flies because he believed salmon fed on butterflies, moths, caterpillars and the like. He was by no means the first fisherman to use highly coloured flies and with a fine lack of logic for one who claimed he was imitating the salmon's natural food, he also explained that salmon became conditioned to taking such flies by their constant use on some rivers.

For centuries up to the 1880s salmon flies were merely big trout flies. The trout fly was developed as an imitation of natural flies. Trout fishermen no doubt saw salmon taking march browns and may flies and certainly hooked salmon when fishing for trout. Younger, a very fine Tweed fisherman, writing in 1839 described the five very plain patterns he used. He wrote of bright flies "like butterflies" which were made in Ireland and which were of little use on the Tweed. He also wrote of salmon taking small trout flies in low water.

Salmon flies then, prior to Kelson's generations, were relatively lightly dressed, some winged, some hackled and mostly dull – flies indeed very much like those we use today for low-water fishing.

Obviously such flies caught fish. Why then did salmon fishermen start using much more heavily dressed, bright coloured flies, and why, if we are to believe Kelson, did these flies outfish the old ones?

On the score of colour, one of the main reasons I feel must have been the greater availability of bright plumage from the East. There is a very natural tendency to suppose that a fly which looks attractive to the human eye has the same appeal to a fish. At this period, too, I think more gentlemen fishermen were tying their own flies. Kelson himself describes the keen angler, puffing away at his after-breakfast pipe and dressing a fly with one eye on the river. Such an angler would be more prone to use one of his own beautiful inventions than some plain concoction of pheasant or turkey and wool or rabbit's fur, dubbed by Jock or Paddy or Dai.

During the last twenty years of the last century too, the fishing-tackle industry was growing apace. The very able businessmen who ran the larger firms in those days knew only too well that tackle caught fishermen as well as fish. Who, except the very knowing, would buy a plain fly when he could purchase, for more money, a gorgeous creation of tinsel and silks, Indian Crow, Macaw, Golden Pheasant and the like. Fishing papers were becoming popular and were eagerly read, providing a medium for Kelson and like enthusiasts to influence opinion and for the Allcocks, Hardys, Farlows, Milwards and many others to reinforce this influence with their advertising. Due partly to the great Fisheries Exhibition, this was a great era of advance in tackle improvement and patent and in specially designed fishing clothing and waders.

These, I am sure, are some of the reasons which produced the heavily dressed gaudy flies which, more slimly dressed, are still in use on most rivers today. These reasons, however, only explain the fly. Why were these flies much more successful than the older plain flies, as they must have been? The answer, I am certain, lies in the great improvements in tackle which took place at this time.

Kelson himself mentions the extra fifteen yards which "modern" tackle allowed over the old hickory rod and line of silk and hair. Although rods were still great beams of 17 and 18 feet weighing about three pounds, they were made from greenheart or split cane and were thus a great advance on the longer, even heavier and weaker rods which were common up until this period. Much more important, lines had improved enormously, and instead of a light line of silk or horse-hair or both, the fisherman had a heavy oil dressed silk line. Kelson mentions cast of over forty yards made with such tackle and using a "Governer", a gadget consisting of a post with a rubber band which held up his back cast, he himself made measured casts of over fifty yards.

You therefore have a situation in which salmon fishermen were reaching out with much longer casts with heavy lines which sank. You have, I submit, the beginnings of sunk line fishing made possible, as was dry fly fishing, by improvements in rods and lines.

Up until these improvements, salmon fly fishing *must* have been a form of "greased line" fishing. With the very long rods capable only of short casts and the very light lines used, the trout-type flies must have been fished very high up in the water. Younger described the rise of the salmon to his flies and the whole technique must have been remarkably similar to modern low-water fishing. Indeed the methods used must have been almost identical with those of two recent masters – Robert Pashley of the Wye and Jack Hughes-Parry of the Welsh Dee. Both used trout rods and light lines fished just under the surface using trout flies. The only difference was that the two modern masters fished from a boat or coracle and the old salmon fishers obtained the same effect with their long rods.

Sunk line fishing was almost impossible before the dressed silk line. The only way to get your fly well down was to cast upstream and poke the rod top right down in the water. This did force the fly down but meant of course that only fish more or less directly below the angler could be covered.

Although Kelson was seeking to imitate some rather vague imaginary salmon food near the surface, he was unintentionally producing a series of good sunk line patterns. Throughout the book he stresses the value of the fly being properly proportioned so that it will swim correctly and not twist unnaturally in the water. Many of the bodies of his flies are of materials which cause them to sink well. Furthermore Kelson writes at some length about "mending" which has come to be associated with Wood and the greased line. When fishing with the well sunk fly I am convinced you cannot fish too slowly and "mending" is much more important in this style of fishing than it is with low-water techniques.

Finally Kelson and his contemporaries were able to throw long lines, without which the fly can never be well sunk. By accident then, and by working on a false premise, he "invented" some excellent patterns for use with this new technique. Your up-to-date fisherman of the 'eighties, however, was not always casting far. Salmon lies were as well defined then as they are now and many must be covered with a shortish cast. Kelson, in his attempt to imitate caterpillars, which he watched salmon eating "through binoculars" – produced the Usk Grub and other similar flies, which are Silhouette flies. You will find Transparent Illusion flies amongst those he lists, and because he understood hackle movement, Normal Image patterns too, and as well, as one would expect, some "flashers". It is of particular interest too that both the Blue Charm and the Logie are listed as good flies on the Dee particularly in low water and on small double hooks. Unfortunately throughout his book Kelson never defines exactly what he means by "small".

The sunk line fly would no doubt have received more attention had its invention not coincided with great improvements in spinning tackle – what was then termed "casting from the reel". Up until the 'eighties spinning for salmon was not greatly practised and the tackle used was fly tackle, with the cast made from coils of line. About the time of Kelson's book, however, the centre-pin reel was being greatly improved; William Shakespeare in the U.S.A. was only ten years away from patenting a level wind multiplier and Malloch was already producing his turn-table reel which was to result in a fully-fledged fixed spool reel, the Illingworth, some twenty years later.

Sunk line fishing, for salmon or for trout, is a difficult technique. To begin with a long line must be cast and controlled – never easy and least of all so with a big fly on the end. Fish, too, are often difficult to hook. It is not surprising that more and more salmon fishermen preferred to master the not-too-easy art of casting a devon or a sprat from these early spinning reels and used this technique in cold, dirty or heavy water.

In consequence the design of the sunk line fly stuck rather fast and apart from having a small spinner incorporated, little was done until very recent times when the Waddington Elverine fly was invented. This is a long, slim "fly" with an articulated body and fitted with a treble hook – a lure which while still difficult to cast, does behave in a most attractive way and does make hooking fish more easy. Somewhat similar is the large tube fly, of which more later.

Although Reg Righyni mentions little of sunk line fishing, a word or two about it is necessary if only because the behaviour of fish to the well sunk fly and to the wooden devon is confirmation of his ideas.

Several authors have stated that it is essential that the sunk fly be fished right on the bottom. On most salmon pools this is quite impossible. The best that can be achieved with a cast which covers the water is to sink the fly down several feet.

In actual fact, as the wooden devon techniques has proved, this is all that is necessary. Only a few years ago, on most salmon rivers in February, unless you were fishing a heavily leaded bait with a lead bumping bottom, you just were not fishing. Now we know that even at the beginning of the season fish "on the take" will come a long way to take an unleaded wooden devon and even when only half or quarter "on" they will still come up some way to intercept a slowly fished lure. It is only when fish are really "off" that it is necessary to fish right on the bottom and this is council of despair. When fish are that "stiff" the only hope is to frighten or annoy one into taking by "bumping him right on the nose".

The sunk line era was a short one and the technique, probably because of its difficulty, never became generally popular. By the early days of the 20th Century, Wood had re-discovered the old method of fly fishing for salmon, which became known as greased line fishing and which led to the low-water fly, sparsely dressed on a long shank hook which we know so well today.

The fact that the conventional low-water fly is not popular on some rivers is surely proof of the soundness of Righyni's reasoning. Obviously the factors controlling acceptance or rejection of a slim fly must be the direction of flow and thus the position of the pools in relation to the sun, and the amount of shade given by trees or by hills. This must account for the effectiveness of "miniature" salmon flies – that is fully dressed flies like Jock Scotts, Thunders and the like in sizes 6, 8, 10, and sometimes 12 – on certain streams.

The latest trend in salmon flies is the tube fly. This is a fly dressed on a plastic or metal tube through which the cast is threaded and tied direct to a very small treble hook. The materials used are both "traditional" – feathers, silks and tinsels – and "new" ones like buck tail, stoat's tail and squirrel. These flies are made in a variety of sizes and shapes and there seems to me great scope for experiment here in design for different light conditions. Personally I do not like tube flies, as I find they are inclined to reverse and catch round the cast. The fact remains that a lot of fish are taken on them.

In Eastern Canada, while the traditional salmon fly is much used, great advances have been made in "primitive" dressings, using hairs and furs readily available in the forests. For many years bucktail flies have been made and at long last hair-wing flies are becoming popular in Britain. Big trout flies are also used in Canada for salmon, but this is a matter of cost, for in Nova Scotia in particular all fishing is free and the poorest can and do fish for salmon.

In Newfoundland some very interesting flies have been developed, using moose hair – a very stiff material indeed. No doubt because of forest-lined banks, some perfect Silhouette flies have been evolved – black, without hackles and with stiff black wings. A great deal of experiment remains to be done over here with materials like moose hair.

The next stage in the development of the salmon fly must be based on the use of hair and fur. These materials are at least as effective as feathers, are much easier to use and cheaper to produce commercially.

Reg writes of the future development of salmon flies being in the hands of the professionals. This I fear is unlikely, for it

149

is fast becoming impossible for a commercial fly-tyer to earn a decent living. Fly dressers are highly skilled workers who require years of training before they can make flies both skilfully and economically. To pay them adequately, on a factory basis at any rate, means offering flies for sale at prices which many fishermen will not pay. It is a strange situation in which an angler will pay a few shillings for a mass-produced spinning bait, but jib at paying the same price for a craft product like a fly.

Final Remarks and a Few Words on Tackle

Perhaps the first, or rather the last, thing to make clear is that none of the three of us who have had a hand in this book, least of all Reg Righyni, believe that anywhere near the last word has been said on any of the ideas put forward. Indeed I am sure that no one would be happier than Reg Righyni to have some of his ideas knocked sideways, provided better ones can be put in their place.

One or two fishermen I know, to whom I have explained the oxygen taking time principle (I refuse to call it a theory any more) have expressed concern that it might take all the "glorious" uncertainty out of salmon fishing. Uncertainty is something I can well do without in fishing, but enough of it will always be there to ensure the fascination. What the taking time principle can do is to allow the fisherman to plan his day according to conditions prevailing. On perfect days, alas! so rare, fish may well be taking all up and down the river at the same time. On the more normal days, taking periods will occur on different pools at different times. It is the fisherman who can work out the best fishing order for the day who will be in the right places at the right time.

The principle, too, does not do away with the value of fishing hard. Reg Righyni rightly points out the dangers of over-fishing lies. Yet the man who has his fly in the water most, in a sensible way, will catch most fish, for there are

150

always those fish who are "quarter on" or "half on". This is one of the reasons why Reg will often counsel you to start off with a spinning rod until things warm up a little and fish come more on the take.

Finally, a word about tackle.

Floating-line fishing for salmon has been altered completely by the invention of the self-floating line. It can no longer be referred to as greased-line fishing because you no longer need grease.

Use a line you can see, preferably a white one. Stifle any prejudice that white will show up to the fish, and take no notice of gillies who tell you it will frighten them. If anything, white will show up less seen from beneath the water against the sky. Frogmen confirm this, but it is not all that important. Salmon may be frightened by a splashing line and are frightened by shadow, but they see so many things floating past on the surface that your line will not bother them. The *important* thing is that you *can see it*, so that you can control it, making your fly fish properly and so that it acts as an indication of a "take".

While this book was being thrashed out, Righyni and I made what we know to be a considerable advance in the design of salmon fly rods. It has always been an advantage at times to use a very light line for salmon – with the advent of the self-floating line, a rod which would handle such light lines became more than ever necessary. True, a powerful trout rod would do the job at times, but even a 10 or 10½-footer left a lot to be desired on all except the smaller rivers. Length means better control, better mending, and better playing of fish, with more line kept out of the water or clear of rocks.

A few years ago, faced with a slightly similar problem to do with float fishing, I patented a rod with a reverse taper in the butt. In other words the cane is thinner at the butt cap than at the top of the handle. Reg is an enthusiast for this type of rod for grayling fishing, and suggested to me that a fly rod on this principle could be the answer to the problem. We also thought such a rod would give greater mending power because of its increased butt flex, and we knew that it would be extremely sensitive.

I made up some rough prototypes, using the staggered ferrule principle, which I believe is the only logical way to make a fly rod of any sort. Making rods with even length joints means having ferrules in the worst possible places. Making a rod with a short butt and joint and a long top greatly improves the balance, action, and increases the sensitivity.

Even the rough prototypes astonished us. With a heavy salmon line they cast a very long line indeed. Yet even with an HDH (Weight Standard 4) line (the equivalent of a No. 2 silk trout line), they gave remarkably efficient casting performance.

The mending and line-placing control was even greater than we had imagined: the extreme sensitivity was there as we had expected, allowing the slightest "touch" to be felt and the finest tackle to be used. The final model, the Flyversa, allows any tackle to be used from medium heavy down to ultra light, gives casting versatility from heavy lines down to very light ones and, most important of all, has that indeterminate thing "feel" which makes all the difference both to efficiency and enjoyment.

In writing this I know I am laying myself open to accusation of self advertising. The whole point of sweating out this book is, we hope, to improve some fisherman's performance and enjoyment. The Flyversa is as much a joint effort in this direction as some of the advice and ideas herein.

Most salmon fishermen in Britain spin to some greater or lesser degree. There is a great deal of skill in good salmon spinning.

If you are going to spin, spin sensibly. The bulk of fishermen use fiddling little seven-foot rods with fixed spool reels, irrespective of the time of year or type of river. Such an outfit does have its place on small rivers and at times of low water.

But just as the short fly rod minimises line control so does the short spinning rod.

Spinning does not consist of casting out your bait and winding it back, although fish are killed in this way. Advanced spinning means controlling the speed and behaviour of the bait by control of the line. You cannot do this with a short rod or a line you cannot see. Use a rod between 8½ and 10 feet, according to conditions and the size of the river. And use a white line.

Index